FOREIGNERS

Stephen
Finucan

PENGUIN
CANADA

PENGUIN CANADA

Published by the Penguin Group

Penguin Books, a division of Pearson Canada, 10 Alcorn Avenue, Toronto, Ontario, Canada M4V 3B2

Penguin Books Ltd, 80 Strand, London WC2R 0RL, England

Penguin Putnam Inc., 375 Hudson Street, New York, New York 10014, U.S.A.

Penguin Books Australia Ltd, 250 Camberwell Road, Camberwell, Victoria 3124, Australia

Penguin Books India (P) Ltd, 11, Community Centre, Panchsheel Park, New Delhi – 110 017, India

Penguin Books (NZ) Ltd, cnr Rosedale and Airborne Roads, Albany, Auckland 1310, New Zealand

Penguin Books (South Africa) (Pty) Ltd, 24 Sturdee Avenue, Rosebank 2196, South Africa

Penguin Books Ltd, Registered Offices: 80 Strand, London WC2R 0RL, England

First published 2003

1 3 5 7 9 10 8 6 4 2

"The Time Before" appeared previously in *Event*.

Publisher's note: This book is a work of fiction. Names, characters, places and incidents either are the product of the author's imagination or are used fictitiously, and any resemblance to actual persons living or dead, events, or locales is entirely coincidental.

Manufactured in Canada.

NATIONAL LIBRARY OF CANADA CATALOGUING IN PUBLICATION DATA

Finucan, Stephen, 1968–
Foreigners : stories / Stephen Finucan.

ISBN 0-14-301219-3

I. Title.

PS8561.I57F67   2003   C813'.6   C2002-905364-1
PR9199.4.F54F67   2003

Visit Penguin Books' website at **www.penguin.ca**

*This book is lovingly dedicated to
the memory of my grandparents*

*Harold Price
&
Grace Frances Price*

He who travels to be amused, or to get somewhat which he
does not carry, travels away from himself, and grows old
even in youth among old things. In Thebes, in Palmyra,
his will and mind have become old and dilapidated as they.
He carries ruins to ruins. Travelling is a fool's paradise.
Our first journeys discover to us the indifference of places.

— Ralph Waldo Emerson
"Self-Reliance"

CONTENTS

ACKNOWLEDGEMENTS

THANKS GO TO MY COMPANIONS on travels both near and far, especially Mark Finucan, Andrew Jefferson, Georgina Kelly, and Jon Lusher. Thanks also to those who offered support and advice along the way: Tara Sweeney, Phil and Lynn Whitaker, Christine Pountney, Michael Limerick, Jeff Wilbee and Ray Roberston. Special thanks to my agent, Anne McDermid, for working so hard, and my editor, Barbara Berson, for making me work so hard. Also, thanks to Cheryl Cohen, whose copy-editing skill made it all sound better.

And always, thanks to my family; without your kindness and love none of this would have been possible.

FOREIGNERS

FOREIGNERS

IN THE MORNINGS HE AWOKE EARLY, just as the sun began to lighten the sky, chasing away the last of the night that in this, the month of April, left behind it a low-lying mist. Slippers on his feet and housecoat wrapped tightly around him, he would pad quietly along the carpeted upstairs hallway to the toilet, which was always cool and drafty no matter the season. There he would shave his face with the old straight razor that had been sharpened so often that its blade was no wider than the thickness of a pencil. He no longer used cake soap, but perfumed foam from a can. His teeth he brushed with powder that the chemist in the village ordered specially. He didn't much like paste, though he kept a tube in the mirrored cabinet above the sink against the eventuality that the powder became unavailable, as had happened with most things he'd grown accustomed to. Afterward, he would dress: white string vest, flannel trousers that had lost their crease, blue collared shirt, the knitted waistcoat that Pippa had

1

made for him the winter before she died, and gabardine
jacket frayed at the cuffs. The waistcoat had gone shabby,
the wool slack, and where the stitches had let loose he'd
done his best to darn them, though the result was a puckered
patchwork of mending.

Then he would walk, wellingtons on his feet: down the
drive and over the road, where he climbed the ladder set
across the stone wall, and on through the field opposite the
farmhouse. It was a good field that drained naturally toward
the woods at its bottom. A path there followed through the
trees, mostly beechnuts and elms, then ran alongside a river
for a mile before turning back on itself and leading once again
to the field.

He'd taken this walk every morning for longer than he
cared to remember. Had taken it even when this field, and
those surrounding it, had belonged to the farm, and when
doing so meant having to put off the chores that needed
tending. Over the years a collection of dogs had accompanied
him. There'd been setters and spaniels, and a skittish terrier
that one day jumped into the river and, having gained the far
shore, ran off never to be seen again. The dog he recalled most
fondly was the last: Duchess, a Labrador retriever bitch that
always dragged a stick along with her wherever she went.
When, the preceding autumn, she'd been run down by a red
Mondeo in the road out front of the farmhouse, he determined that there should be no more after her. He was too old
for a new pup, and too set in his ways to take on a stray from
the RSPCA. Rather, he resigned himself to walking alone.

Making his way back up the slope toward the stone fence,
he thought what a shame it was that the field had gone unused

for so long. Ten years it had been this way, ever since he had sold off the farm's acreage to developers. It was meant to have been turned into a golf course, but the work was never begun. He figured that there must have been trouble with the Ramblers' Society, who no doubt laid claim to the ancient footpath that cut across the two fields above the farmhouse.

He was thinking of this, and about how he was happy that the golf course had not been built, when he took the first rung of the ladder. Then something stopped him: a dark-clad figure standing out front of the farmhouse, face pressed up against the window that gave onto the lounge, hands cupped at the side of the head, so as to get a clear view inside.

He lowered himself back down the ladder and ducked behind the wall. Part of him had been expecting this for some time now, living on his own so far from the village. He was glad he was out of the house; the thought of being done violence terrified him.

He squatted in the wet grass and waited for the sound of shattering glass. How long, he wondered, did it take to burgle a house? Ten minutes? More? These people knew exactly what they were after. Light fare: silver, jewellery, old-age benefit kept in a jar on the countertop, mementos and picture frames that could be pawned in the city. In and out quickly so as not to get caught. That was, of course, unless the intent was merely to do him harm, in which case he would have to remain hidden for some time longer.

It started to rain: a thin drizzle, a cold mist that settled over him like a damp veil. Sitting in the wet grass aggravated his sciatica, and soon the pain shooting down his leg became too much to bear. He stood to stretch it out, and when he did so he glanced over the wall again and saw that the burglar was no longer at the window, but was sitting now on his front doorstep, face in hands, looking altogether pathetic. The sight gave him nerve. He climbed over the ladder and crossed the road. As he came up the drive, though, he began to doubt his impulse and considered that this might have simply been a ploy to get him out into the open where he could be more easily attacked.

As he drew near, the stranger raised her head and revealed a face streaked with blue mascara.

"What the bloody hell do you think you're doing?" he demanded, with more force than he had expected.

"Do you live here?" the woman asked, her voice thick from crying.

"I do," he said, struggling now to keep up his tone. "And I want to know what you think you're playing at?"

She did not reply, just dropped her head again into her hands.

He stood at the stove and heated a tin of beef stew, stirring it more than was necessary. She sat at the table behind him, hands wrapped tightly around her mug of tea, her face tipped forward into the rising steam. Every so often he moved to the sideboard on the pretense of arranging the crockery or cutting brea or setting out the salt and pepper so that he might steal another look at her. She still wore her dark blue anorak, wet with rain and dripping on the floor. Below that, black jeans and scruffy white trainers. She was, he decided, in her mid- to late thirties, possibly even forty, but surely no older. Her hair was short, thick and dark; black almost as Duchess's coat, with no hint of grey. He thought it likely dyed, being that it was a shade or two darker than her eyebrows. Her skin contrasted sharply: pale; not alabaster, but ashen. Except for beneath her eyes, where it deepened almost to purple. At first he'd considered this a result of the smudged mascara, but the colour remained even after she'd dried her eyes. Then he recognized it to be the bruising of exhaustion. Pippa's complexion had taken on a similar aspect in her final months, when she began to fear sleep.

He finished buttering two thick slices of bakery bread and set them on a plate. Then he turned off the gas ring and removed the pot from the stove-top. As he portioned the stew into bowls, he made certain that the extra ladle went into his own. He placed a bowl before her, and she mumbled a thank you but did not look up from the table. She appeared wary of him, of his generosity, though he could see no good reason why. If anyone should be uncomfortable, he felt it should be himself. He was the one who had taken a stranger, a peeper, quite possibly a person bent on criminal intent, into his home. Who was to say she did not have a partner lurking about outside, awaiting the signal to burst through the door and batter him senseless? Though he had to admit, the likelihood seemed remote. To look at her, she seemed more apt to do harm to herself than to him.

"It's all right, is it?" he asked, sitting opposite her as she greedily spooned the stew into her mouth.

She glanced up quickly, somewhat embarrassed as she raised a hand to her lips to stifle a small belch.

"Yes, thank you," she said, averting her eyes again. "I'm sorry. My manners. It's just that I'm so very hungry. I've not eaten since the day before yesterday."

"That's quite a while," he said, carefully lifting a spoonful of stew and blowing on it before eating.

"I'd a cheese and pickle sandwich," she offered. "From a machine at Derby Station."

"Derby's a long way from here."

"Yes," she said and continued eating.

Her name was Marion. She was married. Her husband was in London, but of that she would say no more. She'd left two weeks before. A coach from Victoria Station had taken her to Torquay, where she'd stayed in a small seaside hotel until her money ran short. With her remaining pounds, she purchased a one-way rail ticket as far as Derby. After Derby, she walked. As for reasons, she did not offer any, and he did not press. One further piece of information did, however, come to light, though she remained unaware of it. He perceived it in her voice; it was not the words she spoke, but the manner in which they were spoken. There was a sharpness to her vowels that she could not quite hide. Her borrowed English inflections could not completely conceal her original accent. In her voice he recognized himself: that slow progression in his speech patterns that over time made his tongue all but indistinguishable from those he lived among. Only a keen ear could discern his foreignness any more, as his keen ear had discerned hers. But he said nothing to her of this, not wishing to establish a confidence.

When she finished eating, he gathered their bowls and rinsed them in the sink. Outside the skies had opened and heavy raindrops streaked the kitchen window. He began to consider how he might broach the subject of her leaving. Her presence unsettled him and he distrusted her story. That she'd so easily admitted to having no money made him suspicious. But when he turned back to the table he found that she'd fallen asleep, sitting upright in the chair. Her head drooped forward; she was snoring softly. He looked out the window again. Already the rain was forming into puddles on the drive.

He walked around the table and gently nudged her shoulder. She looked up at him in alarm.

"You seem rather worn out," he said, trying not to sound too concerned. "If you'd like, you can rest here a while before carrying on your way."

"That's very kind of you," she said, smiling for the first time. "Only if it's not too much trouble."

He led her upstairs to the guest room. It was the room in which Pippa's mother had stayed until he and Pippa moved her into the nursing home. At one time they'd imagined it would become a nursery.

"It might be a little musty," he said. "You may want to open a window."

"I'm sure it will be fine," she replied. She closed the door behind her.

He spent that afternoon as he spent most afternoons. First it was a nature documentary on BBC2, followed by the *One O'Clock News*. An arts program on Radio Four filled the

silence while he fitted pieces into a jigsaw of Westminster
Abbey; it was the third time he'd done the puzzle. If he
managed to finish it before the end of the week he would
allow himself to purchase a new one from the newsagent's in
the village.

At half three he gathered up the loose tiles and returned
them to the box. After which he sat himself in his armchair
beside the window in the lounge to read. But when he picked
up the book from the side table, he discovered that he'd
neglected to mark the page, and try as he might, he could not
find where he'd left off the previous afternoon. So he set the
novel aside and gazed out the window.

He saw the smudge on the pane: the greasy stain left behind
when she pressed her nose and forehead to the glass. He
looked toward the ceiling. Not a sound had come from
upstairs since she'd closed the door on him. She'd been so
quiet that he had half forgotten he was not alone in the house.
He found the thought of this disconcerting.

She must be made to leave, he decided, and the sooner the
better. He realized, however, that it was now more than simply
a question of turning her out, though in all honesty he knew
that he had already done far more than was to be expected.
After some consideration, he resolved to give her thirty quid
and pay for a taxi to take her to the village. If she liked, she
could use the money for a bed and breakfast or to buy a coach
ticket to Derby or London, or wherever it was she needed to
get to. It made no difference to him, just as long as she was gone.

He left her to sleep while he arranged things. He found the
number of a minicab company in the telephone directory and
wrote it down on a pad of paper. Then, as a gesture of added

generosity, he retrieved two twenty-pound notes from the jar on the countertop and laid them on the table beside the telephone.

When the hour came that he usually sat down in front of the television to have his tea, he climbed the stairs to wake her. At the door to the bedroom he felt a flutter of nervousness and had to wait a moment before knocking. When no answer came, he tapped a little louder. Still receiving no reply, he turned the handle and gently pushed open the door.

The first thing he noticed was that she had laid her clothes out over the floor. It was almost as if as she'd shed her wet layers as she made her way across the room. But the garments were not strewn haphazardly. Instead, they were neatly stretched out so as to avoid wrinkling as they dried. He was careful not to tread on anything as he walked over to the bed.

She stirred as he approached, rolling onto her side. As she did, the duvet fell away and revealed to him a naked breast. For a moment he was transfixed. The soft, pale flesh; the blue faintness of veins around the brown bruise of her nipple. She murmured something he could not understand; moaned softly.

Slowly he reached out and took hold of a corner of the duvet and covered her again. Then he turned and left the room.

———⁓———

He was disappointed to find her sitting at the kitchen table when he came downstairs the following morning. She'd made herself a cup of tea and was smoking a cigarette, the ashes of which she flicked into a saucer.

"I'm sorry," she said, extinguishing the cigarette. "I couldn't find an ashtray."

"I haven't any," he replied, picking up the saucer and depositing her fag-ends in the bin before rinsing the plate clean. "Got rid of them years ago."

"You gave up smoking, then," she said, trying to sound cheerful.

"I've never smoked."

He turned and faced her. She looked different to him: healthier, less fraught. He felt strangely guilty for having been harsh.

"My wife did, though," he added. "When she was still alive."

"I see," she said.

He wondered if she did. He'd not been trying to imply that cigarette smoking had caused Pippa's death; he'd simply said it for the sake of saying something. Although now he wondered why he had bothered. For the remark seemed to be having a wounding effect, and the slight trace of colour he'd seen in her cheeks a moment earlier drained away. An awkward silence descended. He thought now might be the time to bring up her leaving, but she spoke before he had the chance.

"It was awfully kind of you to take me in like that," she said, trying to muster a smile again. "I can't believe I slept so long."

"You must have been quite tired."

"Oh, yes. Yes, I was." Her voice brightened and she sat forward in her chair. "I didn't know it myself, but I truly was. I think I was asleep as soon as my head touched the pillow. I didn't move a muscle until I woke up this morning."

He looked past her to the telephone table. The two twenty-pound notes and the paper with the number of the minicab company lay undisturbed.

"It's the fresh air," he said. "It tires one out."

"It sure does," she replied. "I've always thought that odd. You would expect it to be invigorating, seeing that it's so clean and . . . well, fresh."

It seemed to him, now that she was rested, that she was eager to talk. He wished she wouldn't. He had grown accustomed to silence, and the thought of having to fill it taxed him. When he gave no indication of wanting to carry on the conversation, she took up the mantle herself.

"You've got a lovely farm," she said, attempting to draw him out.

"It's not a farm. Not any more, at least."

"Really?" she said.

"The land's all sold off," he said and walked into the mud room to find his wellingtons.

When he returned, a look of pity had settled over her. As he sat down at the table to pull on his boots, she leaned slightly toward him.

"That must have been very sad for you," she said, sympathetically. "Having to sell your land, I mean."

"Was never really mine," he said, bent over his boots. "Belonged to my wife's family. I was never much of a farmer. Truth is, I was glad to be rid of it. Always was too much work for one man."

"What did you have?" she asked. "I mean, was it crops? Livestock?"

"Beef cattle first," he replied, absently. "Sheep for a while after that. Nothing much near the end."

"And you did it for your wife."

Now he looked at her, annoyed that he had allowed himself to be taken in by her talk.

"She must have been quite special," she said after a moment. "For you to keep a farm going when you really didn't want to."

He stood up from the table and turned toward the door.

"I'm going for my walk now," he said, coolly. "I walk every morning."

"I wonder," she said before he could add anything, "would you mind so much if I used your bath? It's just that I haven't had a proper wash since I left the hotel in Torquay. Days ago now."

He did not look at her when he spoke: "You'll find the bathroom at the top of the stairs to your right, beside the toilet. Towels are in the linen cupboard just inside the door."

—⚬—

He first came to the farm with Pippa on their honeymoon. Two days were all they'd been given, and all things considered, even that was generous. They'd been hastily married by the base chaplain at Aldershot, who, before he joined them, reiterated his disapproval of wartime marriages. Her parents had not been able to attend. So it was decided that rather than Land's End, as they had planned, they would go north to the farm.

For a few delirious days, Pippa's mother paraded him around all the shops in the village, fawning, almost flirtatious, in her delight. Showing him off like a trophy to all, and running her hand proudly over the shoulder flashes of his dress uniform.

At the farm, two evacuee children from Whitechapel, whom Pippa's parents were fostering, followed him around; as he pitched in awkwardly with the chores, they laughed at his clumsiness and strange accent. Even Pippa's father, whose weak heart left him able to only direct the young boys in the farm work, smiled at his well-intentioned but feeble efforts at mucking out the cowsheds.

They were given the guest room, the two boys being made to share the narrow bed in Pippa's own room. Their first night together as man and wife, Pippa allowed him to undress her. She stood beside the bed, eyes closed, a faint smile curling her lips, as he unbuttoned her skirt and let it fall to the floor. Her blouse, once opened, he pushed gently from her shoulders. He unfastened her stockings from her garters one at a time and rolled them down her soft white legs; she put her hands on his shoulders as he slipped them from her feet. She lay down on the bed then and raised her hips so he could remove her knickers. She reached around and unclasped her brassiere as he climbed in beside her. They made love quietly; the only sound, the voices of her parents talking to one another in the next room.

Later, after Pippa had fallen asleep, he got out of bed and sat in a chair by the window. The entire house was silent then as he watched her sleep. The bedclothes were gathered around her hips and her bare torso was lit by the moonlight through the window. It was a clear, starry night. There would be air raids over the cities: Liverpool, Birmingham, Hull, London. But there, in the quiet countryside, watching Pippa as she slept, he did not care.

It had been such a very long time since he'd thought of that night. And as he stood now, in the middle of the field, the slate grey sky again threatened rain.

He stood in the doorway to the kitchen and watched as she buttered toast on the sideboard. On the countertop beside her lay his library book. She put the knife down, licked the tip of her finger and turned a page, still unaware of his presence. He retreated into the mud room and opened the outside door, then slammed it shut again. He took his time removing his boots.

When he re-entered the kitchen she had set the book aside and was standing by the table, in her hands a plate piled high with toast.

"What's all this, then?" he asked.

"You've just been so kind," she said, sounding very pleased with herself, "that I thought I would do something nice for you." She put the plate down on the table, which had been set with cutlery, paper napkins, salt and pepper, brown sauce and red. "I found some side bacon and eggs in the fridge. And a can of baked beans in the larder." She took a dishtowel from the counter and moved to the stove. From the oven she retrieved the two plates she'd left to warm. "I thought you would be back sooner. I didn't want everything going cold."

She set the plates down on the table and smiled at him. He'd not come any farther into the kitchen.

"I hope you don't mind," she said.

"I was saving that for my Sunday tea," he replied.

"Oh."

She looked at the table, then back to him.

"I should have waited," she said.

"Yes," he said. "You should have."

Even as he spoke, he could see the tears beginning to well in her eyes. She wiped them away quickly with the back of her hand.

"You're right," she said. "It was presumptuous of me." She folded the towel into a neat square and set it down on the table. "I should go, I think." She looked at him; her smile waned. "You've been very good."

For a moment he felt quite weak and thought he might have to put a hand against the wall to steady himself.

"I've left a few things upstairs," she said, moving toward the hallway. "I'll just collect them and be on my way."

He remained where he was, listening to her footsteps as they made their way up the stairs and along the corridor. He could hear her moving about in the room above. Then came the sound of the bedroom door being closed. She was carrying a small black haversack when she came back into the kitchen. He'd not noticed it before; she must have worn it under her anorak. She stood for a moment looking at him, as if searching for something to say, then turned to go.

"Wait," he said.

She stopped, but did not face him.

"It seems such a waste," he said, crossing to the sideboard where he opened a narrow cupboard. "You've gone to the trouble of making a meal; it would be silly not to eat it." He withdrew two dinner trays and brought them to the table. "I'll never be able to finish all of this myself," he said, as he began to load the plates onto the tray. "Please stay."

Now she turned.

"Are you sure?" she asked, her voice uncertain.

It was his turn to smile.

"Of course," he said, trying to sound casual. "Besides, I couldn't send you off on an empty stomach."

He held out a tray to her.

"I hope it's all right," he said, "but I prefer to eat in the lounge."

—⁂—

They ate in silence, and afterward he collected both trays and took them to the kitchen. Then he set about making a pot of tea, which he carried back into the lounge with the china service Pippa always saved for special occasions. He'd had to fetch it down from a top shelf in the cupboard and wipe away the dust. He also brought along an extra saucer for her to use as an ashtray.

She was standing beside the settee when he returned, looking at a small silver-framed photograph hanging on the wall. It was the picture taken of him and Pippa immediately after their wedding ceremony, just before they left for the station to come to the farm. It had been a windy day, and in the photo Pippa had to hold her nurse's cap on with her hand because she'd misplaced her hatpin. They were both laughing at something that had been said, but he could no longer remember what it was. They were standing outside the base chapel, and if one looked closely, the chaplain's pinched face could be seen peering through a small window on the far right.

"That's you and your wife, is it?" she asked, leaning in close to the photograph.

"Yes," he said as he set the service down on the coffee table. "We were just married."

"She's very beautiful."

"Yes. She was."

He poured out the tea. "Do you take sugar?" he asked.

"Just a little milk, thank you."

She sat down on the settee and he passed her a cup. After she'd taken it, he set the extra saucer at the edge of the table and nodded toward it.

"Are you sure you don't mind?" she asked.

"No, not at all." He took his own cup and sat again in the chair beside the window. He watched her as she took a packet of cigarettes from the pocket of her anorak, which she'd laid over the arm of the settee. She withdrew one and lit it with a slim gold lighter, then tipped her head back and blew a thin cloud of smoke toward the ceiling. He seemed unable now to take his eyes off her, and as he brought his cup to his lips, he slightly misjudged the distance and spilled a drop of tea down his front. This brought a smile to her face.

"What was her name?" she asked, picking up her cup and saucer while still holding the cigarette between her fingers.

"Pippa," he said. "Philippa, actually."

"That's a lovely name."

He nodded and glanced up at the photograph.

"How," she said, "if you don't mind my asking, did you meet?"

He set his cup down on the side table and folded his hands in his lap. She was perched on the edge of the settee, an almost childlike glint in her eyes.

"Ah, well, yes," he said and brushed a piece of lint from his trousers.

"If you'd rather not, that's fine."

"No, it's perfectly all right," he said. "Just not much of a story, really. I was a second lieutenant in the Sixth Infantry.

We were stationed at Aldershot, down south. Training for the Normandy invasion, as it turned out; though we'd no idea of it at the time. Pippa was a nursing sister in the British Army Surgical Hospital at Newdigate."

"You were wounded?" she asked, concerned.

He was amused by her worried tone, so long after the fact, and felt a flickering of emotion for her.

"No," he continued. "Not wounded, per se—unless you consider appendicitis a wound. I was operated on at Newdigate. Philippa was on the recovery ward. Sounds romantic, I know, but in truth, it was all rather messy. Bedpans and sick and what have you. But that didn't put her off. We were married after I was released from hospital."

She took one more puff of her cigarette before stubbing it out in the saucer, then sat back on the settee. Her face became gloomy.

"It must have been so awful for you."

He wrinkled his brow: "How do you mean?"

"France. Normandy. Those terrible beaches."

"Oh, I never went to France. Not long after that photo was taken," he said, pointing over her shoulder, "I contracted peritonitis. Spent most of the duration of the war in an invalid hospital."

—⁓—

She was curious and wanted to see the farm. He told her there wasn't much left worth looking at, but she was insistent, and it made him rather prideful. First they crossed the yard to the one remaining outbuilding, but she seemed disappointed when he explained that it wasn't anything more than a storage shed; he'd kept winter feed in it at one point, but now only used it to store old garden tools and other such rubbish. The foundation for the barn was also rather a letdown. He'd sold the slate roof tiles to a salvage company from Matlock and had the walls knocked down after they became something of an eyesore to him.

She perked up a bit when he pulled back the rusty gate and led her through to the paddock. The grasses had already grown knee-high and here and there among the nettles beechnut saplings had begun to take root. He pointed them out to her and explained that the sheep would have eaten them long before they reached such a height; that, in fact, they'd have eaten everything to the ground, nettles included.

At the top of the paddock was the one remaining cattle shelter; the other, which stood on the opposite side of the stone wall that separated the paddock from the upper field, had collapsed three winters before. He showed her the long trough where he used to feed the sheep, and the cattle before them, as well as the remnants of a salt lick that had melted away over the years, staining the concrete floor of the shelter a pale violet blue.

She ran the toe of her trainer through the powdery blemish, then walked on to the stone wall. He stood back a moment, watching her. She leaned on her elbows and stared out over the field. A slight breeze coming from behind ruffled her short hair, revealing the pale nape of her neck. He went and stood beside her.

"This wall could do with mending," he said, rocking a loose stone on its top. "I've let things go a bit."

"It does seem a shame," she said.

"Well, it's not such an easy job for me any more. I'd have to take it down to its base to fix it properly."

"No," she said, turning to him. "I mean this." She nodded toward the field.

"Ah, yes," he agreed. "I think so, too, at times. But things change."

"For the better?" she asked.

"Sometimes yes, sometimes no," he smiled. "This time, I think yes."

She looked away again. She seemed unconvinced.

"Tell me," she said. "Is it lonely?"

He shrugged his shoulders; he'd never thought so before. Then he turned and started back down the paddock. "Come with me," he called over his shoulder. "I've something I want to show you."

He could not recall the last time he had looked at them, and for a moment was panicked when they were not on the shelf in the lounge where he'd thought. Finally, after some rummaging, he found the small black cardboard box with the silver lettering that read *Pepper & Sons* in the bottom drawer of the bureau, beneath Pippa's mother's lace tablecloth.

He left the drawer hanging open and went and sat next to her on the settee. He put the box down on the coffee table and took a deep breath.

"She was very angry with me when I gave them to her," he said, sounding slightly mischievous. "I drove all the way to Birmingham to have them made. I was told by someone in the village, I can't remember who, that Birmingham was the place."

Very carefully, he lifted the lid from the box and set it aside. Then he folded back the tissue paper. She had to lean forward to see what was inside.

"My God, they're beautiful."

He grinned: "Go on, take them out."

He watched her as she dipped her slender fingers into the box and gently removed the two rings. She then placed them in the palm of her hand.

"For a long time," he said, "we had very little money. When we were married I gave her a copper band, which was itself hard to come by. It always turned her finger green. There was never any thought of an engagement ring."

"How could she ever have been angry with you?"

"Well, as I said, we hadn't a lot of money really, even then. Truth be told," he continued, "I'd been putting little bits away for a few years before I bought them." Now he laughed: "And when I did finally give them to Pippa, she was so upset with me that she refused to wear them."

"Really?"

"Oh, it didn't last. Once she let me put them on her finger she never took them off. Not even when she was doing the washing up, which made me rather nervous."

She slipped the rings, a small diamond solitaire in a raised setting and a gold band with delicate scrolling, onto her bare ring finger and held her hand out in front of her.

"I don't blame her," she said. "Though I can understand your being worried."

As she removed them she noticed that the width of each had been slightly altered, thin cuts where a dull metal had been added.

"Were they too small for her?" she asked.

"Oh, that," he said, taking the rings from her and returning them to the box. "That's nothing."

She placed a hand on his forearm. "I'm glad you showed them to me."

"Yes," he said, rising quickly from the settee. "Yes, I just thought you might like to see them."

He walked back to the bureau and put the box in the drawer. He straightened the folds in the tablecloth and laid it carefully on top.

—⁂—

They fitted the last piece into the jigsaw puzzle of Westminster Abbey shortly before three and then, at her insistence, he napped in his chair in the lounge while she set about preparing tea. He slept soundly and woke refreshed, if a little stiff-necked, to a meal the likes of which he'd not had in a very long time: roast chicken, parsnips, potatoes, Brussels sprouts, boiled carrots and pork sausage. They ate not in the lounge, but at the dining-room table. They finished with cups of coffee and ice cream from a tub she'd found at the bottom of the deep freeze, where the chicken had lain hidden for so long. They did the washing up together. And afterward he took down two tumblers from the cupboard and brought them into the lounge, along with the bottle of cognac he kept now for whenever he felt a cold coming on.

First they watched a comedy program that he did not fully understand, but it made her laugh so he said nothing. Then it was time for the *Nine O'Clock News*. As the presenter began with a story on the Middle East, he wondered how it was that the evening had passed so quickly. He poured himself a second glass of cognac.

"I sometimes think," he said, "that the world has gone quite mad."

The third story was that of a pensioner, an eighty-one-year-old widow in Luton, who'd been attacked by two men who followed her home from the post office after she'd cashed her benefit cheque. They'd tied her to a chair and beat her with a blackjack until her eyes had swollen shut. Then they'd used old newspapers to set fire to her settee and left her to die. Neighbours had heard the struggle, but none called for help until they saw smoke billowing from the window of her council house. All were shocked that such a thing could happen. A photograph of the woman in hospital, bandages covering her face, was shown. Police had no leads in the case, but were confident that the perpetrators would be found.

"You're right," she said. "Quite mad."

As the main news switched over to the East Midlands broadcast he leaned back in the chair and watched her. He felt slightly light-headed from the cognac. She was sitting forward on the settee; her glass, only half-drunk, she rolled between her palms, every once in a while taking the smallest of sips, at which she wrinkled her nose. Looking at her in profile as she eyed the television, he wondered if he didn't see something of Pippa in her. In the line of her jaw, possibly, which stood out strongly from her thin neck; or in the smallness of her ears. Pippa had had tiny ears, with only the hint of a lobe. Often he'd teased her about them by talking more loudly than was necessary.

When she turned to him he was smiling.

"Is there something funny?" she asked, returning his grin.

"No, no," he said, shaking his head. "I was just thinking."

"What about?"

"Nothing in particular, really," he said. "Least ways nothing of interest." He held out the bottle. "Would you like a top-up?"

"No, thank you. I'm fine."

She set her glass on the table. "In fact," she said, getting to her feet. "I think I might turn in if it's all the same to you. It's been a long day."

———⁓———

It used to be that he would have a glass of cognac every night before bed, to help him off to sleep, until the time came when he found that even this small tipple left him groggy the following morning. But now, nearing the bottom of his third, he was looking forward to a fourth.

The empty Pepper & Sons box lay on the table beside him and he held the rings in his hand. The jeweller who'd mended them had done a poor job. The director of the funeral parlour had been apologetic about having to cut them from Pippa's finger and quite kindly offered to pay part of the repair cost, but he'd refused. And when he drove with them all the way back to Birmingham he found that Pepper & Sons was no longer in business. It had become a museum. The woman who ran the gift shop suggested he take them to a jeweller in the city centre. The address she gave him was that of a shabby storefront shop whose proprietor offered to buy both rings. When he wouldn't sell, the man suggested that he at least replace the stone in the engagement ring, informing him that the original was of deficient calibre. In the end he took them to the local jeweller in the village who did the job for him at half price.

He laid the rings back in the box and poured himself another measure of cognac, which he carried across the room. Standing beside the settee he looked at the photograph of himself and Pippa. Before that afternoon it had been some time since he had taken notice of it. And staring at it now, he realized that he had forgotten how young Pippa once was. Most often when he thought about her, it was as she was near the end: her bones brittle from the osteoporosis, her heart congestive like her father's and her mind ruined by the dementia that robbed him of her even before she died. In those last months, he remembered her walking the darkened house at night, unable to sleep, not recognizing him when he came to take her back to bed. A different Pippa from the one in the photograph, from the laughing girl who had to hold her hat on in the wind. He took a drink of cognac and held it in his mouth until it burned his tongue.

He stood in the open doorway and watched her as she slept. The light from the hallway splashed across the floor. She had folded her clothes and laid them on the chair beside the window. In bed she lay with her head turned away from him, facing the wall. Through the duvet, which was pulled tight under her chin, he could see the shape of her breasts, rising and falling in the slow motion of slumber.

He took a step forward and plunged the room into darkness. He listened to her breathing: measured, constant. When he stepped back, the light returned, illuminating her again. He remained a moment longer, watching her, then pulled the door closed.

—⁓—

In the night he dreamed that she crept into his room and stood naked at the foot of his bed. She was lit by moonlight. When he pulled back the duvet she slipped into the bed beside him, pressed herself against his tired body. He took her breast in his mouth, tasted the warmth of her flesh, the distant saltiness of her skin. In his dream she did not speak, just a faint smile curling her lips. Then the brightness woke him and he felt spent. It was late, the morning sun already high.

He stood before the mirror in his bedroom and dressed himself. As he buttoned his waistcoat, he found that another stitch had come loose. It would need to be mended before it could unravel further. After his walk, he decided: a cup of tea, the darning needle; maybe he would watch some television as he set about it.

The faintest trace of cigarette smoke greeted him in the kitchen, but nothing else. No empty teacup; no saucer with fag-ends. The money was gone from the telephone table, but the number for the minicab company had been left behind.

In the lounge he found his empty glass and the bottle of cognac where he had left it on the side table beside the Pepper & Sons box. He sat down and filled the glass halfway and looked out the window. The previous day's rain had not quite washed away the stain her face had left on the pane. He saw through it to the field across the road, brilliant green in the bright morning sun. He brought the glass to his lips and drank, feeling the warmth of the cognac as it slid down his throat into his empty belly. It settled there like a small fire.

He set the glass back down and picked up the box. He turned it over in his hands several times, tracing his finger along the edges before opening it, though he needn't have bothered. He knew by the weight alone that the rings were gone. Sitting there, he remembered how they had looked on her slender, bare finger. She could get a fair price for them from any pawnbroker. They were of good quality, no matter what the Birmingham jeweller had said, and they would take her as far as she needed to go.

DEVIL WITHIN

MARLOWE TOOK ILL and had to remain at the Excelsior while I went on alone. It wasn't meant to be that way. Marlowe was the one who had found them eight months earlier. And while it was true that I had Mathieu at my disposal, I lacked any field experience. Marlowe had come to refer to me, only half jokingly, as the lab rat. I spent my time at the institute hunched over a microscope, examining samples taken from the brains of the smaller primates. I crunched the data and catalogued the specimens that Marlowe brought back from his expeditions. I compiled neat reports culled from his often chaotic field journals and presented his findings to the Board of Governors, ensuring that he would have the funding required for his next junket. I was very good when it came to the bureaucratic and experimental minutiae; in other words, those aspects of the work that Marlowe abhorred. In truth, he was not a man given to such things, being far too gregarious. I, on the other hand, was mundane: perfectly suited. And though Marlowe at times chided me for being so, I think there was a small part of him that was jealous of my institutional abilities.

Still, I must admit that in the back of my mind I'd always harboured fantasies of working in the field. Vague and romanticized notions of bivouacking in the wilds, only the humming hurricane lamps to fend off the blackness of a jungle night; of constructing a crude block and tackle to lift myself into the Amazonian canopy where I would locate a new and healing subspecies of orchid; of hacking my way through the near-impenetrable bush of a torrid equatorial clime to discover a tribe long thought vanished. But even I knew that these were flights of fancy, beyond me in real life if not simply because of my disposition, then certainly because of my age. Marlowe had fifteen years on me; and there were those who had fifteen years on Marlowe. And yet, he'd found his lost tribe.

Strictly speaking, though, the people in the village of Ascension were neither lost nor a tribe, but a people living apart. If that constituted a tribe, then one could say that I was myself a tribe, Marlowe too. Ascension lay high in the mountains of the Maladif district, the only region in this island nation still covered by the dense forest that once blanketed the entire country. Everywhere else the jungle had been denuded. First it was for the rich mahogany; international lumber companies clear-cut entire districts so that the wealthy could furnish their homes with the dark red wood. What they left the peasants stripped away and baked into charcoal to be sold at the markets in the cities along the coast. The rainy seasons took care of the rest, washing away the fertile soil so all that remained were the scarred and scrubby reminders of what once was. All, that is, except for the Maladif district, whose hills lay lush and foreboding.

People here are afraid of the jungle of the Maladif district. Even Mathieu, who was born in a town in the foothills there, expressed his wariness at venturing too far into the forest. "It is a bad place," Mathieu said. "Bad things happen there." Bad things, many believed, that were perpetrated by the villagers of Ascension.

That didn't stop Mathieu from taking the money Marlowe offered him. His initial cockiness, when he assured us that he could lead us directly to the village, only waned as our departure neared. I felt certain, as I'm sure Marlowe did, that Mathieu would abandon us soon after we entered the jungle; that at the first opportunity he would make his escape and return to the capital to revel in his triumph, regaling his mates with the story of how he cheated the *blancs* and left them to wander in the *mal-foret*.

I hadn't been that bothered by the prospect at first. I figured that even if Mathieu did abscond, Marlowe could get us to Ascension. But now that he was laid up in the Excelsior, I would be left to the mercy of Mathieu. When I tried to explain my concern to Marlowe, he would not hear it.

"Don't be such a fool, James," he said to me, lifting himself from his fever-stained sheets. "He wouldn't think of leaving you out there. Especially not as I'll be here in Cap Gloire. It would take very little effort to locate him in the event that he returned without you. What guides there are hereabouts spend their days drinking *usque* in the cantinas down along the quay. In any case, Mathieu is well aware that it would only take a word to my friends in the *Force Sûreté* to have him taken care of."

It was Marlowe's relationships with members of the new
regime that had afforded us the opportunity to be the first to
approach the villagers of Ascension. I do not know upon what
these relationships were based or how they were first estab-
lished. Marlowe didn't think it necessary to tell me. I'm sure
it had to do with money somewhere along the line. For as
Marlowe explained to me several times, in this country all
dealings with the government are effected by bribery.
Corruption is the mainstay.

Yet there seemed something more to Marlowe's relation-
ship with the officials here. The deputy minister of the
Interior greeted our arrival at the airport, and when he
welcomed Marlowe, he did so with a reverence that seemed
disproportionate. I also detected a slight hint of fear in the
man's aspect; nebulous, but nonetheless apparent. Maybe it
had something to do with the fact that the deputy minister,
unlike the majority of the officers who'd carried out the most
recent coup, was not a native of the Maladif district. This was
unusual, since it is the tendency in this country for usurpers of
power—here it is usually the case of one junta overthrowing
another—to adhere to a geographic loyalty rather than one
based on rank. For example, the previous military government
comprised, to a man, officers from Marais, the western-most
district of the country. Marlowe made certain I did my reading
before we arrived.

Still, friendship with the authorities alone could not
guarantee exclusivity. After the doctor had left us—warning
Marlowe that if he did not remain in bed and allow the
antibiotics to run their course, the virus would strip the cilia
from the walls of his intestines—I did my best to convince

him that the excursion should be postponed. I advised that
we wait until he was back on his feet.

"This is your project," I said to him. "You've put in the
work."

Again he would not hear of it.

"What you've got to understand, James," he told me,
taking hold of my left hand to quell its slight tremor, "is that
here corruption is simply a way of life. My friends have been
kind enough to grant us a head start. But the bribery has
begun. The pharmaceutical companies have reached deep
into their pockets. Palms, as they say, have already been
greased. At the least, we have a week's advantage. My friends
can delay the paperwork only so long. As for me, I could be
laid up here for months. If you don't go now, then we'll have
missed our chance."

Of course, I knew he was right. I knew that I had no choice
but to forge ahead without him.

—⁂—

The roads in Cap Gloire were miserable, the potholes unlike
anything I had experienced. It was as if great starving beasts
had fed upon the asphalt. There was no driving over these
craters. Instead, motorists, cyclists and pedestrians alike gave
them wide berth, as though in venturing too close one ran the
risk of being swallowed up by the earth itself. I noticed this
soon after we'd passed through the front gates of the Excelsior,
Mathieu behind the wheel of the open-topped Land Rover
that Marlowe had managed to secure for us, courtesy of one of
his friends in the *Force Sûreté*. As we made our way along
Avenue-de-la-Mer, heading north away from the ocean and

toward the highway that would lead us into the interior, I glanced over my shoulder to get a last look at the Excelsior.

L'Hôtel Excelsior had been everything and nothing like what I'd expected. I was somewhat disappointed when Marlowe told me that we would be staying there. The romantic fantasies again. What I'd desired was a rough base camp in the countryside, or at the very least some sort of wilderness station: a place that occupied that netherworld between civilization and the bush. I freely admit that I conjured these images from the darkened cinemas of my childhood: films of African safaris and colonial wars. I wanted dusty, clapboard buildings with gaps in the walls that allowed the whistling wind to blow through; or better still, a ring of squarish canvas tents, all facing in toward a great roaring fire, the only amenity a jerry-rigged bush shower with a tarpaulin curtain and a bucket with holes drilled in the bottom. I said no such thing to Marlowe, of course, not wanting to draw any more attention to my inexperience. Still, I have no doubt that my chagrin was evident when we arrived at the hotel.

There was a time when the Excelsior rivalled, if not in size, most definitely in splendour, the grand resorts of the French Riviera, on which it was modelled. Rising majestically from behind a tall greystone wall, it stood as a rose-coloured paragon to the wealthy Europeans and Americans who paid exorbitant prices to occupy one of its sixty-five rooms, each a fully furnished suite with canopy bed and sunken bathtub. On the ocean side of the hotel a wide white-sand beach, restricted to guests, led down to the turquoise waters of Baie de Gloire. There were red-clay tennis courts to one side, and to the other a palm-shaded swimming pool, the bottom of which was inlaid with a ceramic mural depicting the hotel itself. The courtyard contained a magnificent tropical garden displaying a collection of colourful blooms indigenous to the island: jacaranda, giant poinsettia, hibiscus and flowering frangipani.

But that was the Excelsior in its heyday. The Excelsior that now stood at the foot of Avenue-de-la-Mer was but a shadow of its former self. Rolls of concertina wire now coiled across the top of the greystone wall, there to prevent thieves from stealing in and robbing the guests as they slept. The facade had bleached to a pale, unhealthy pink, and in places the stucco had come away altogether, leaving angry white scars. The pool was dry and its tiles cracked, the nets were gone from the tennis courts and the beach was befouled by the detritus of the poor, who squatted by the water's edge in the hope of salvaging something of value from the jetsam offered up by the torpid sea. The only part of the Excelsior that in any way resembled its former glory was its lounge. The bar at the Excelsior had always been the centre of Cap Gloire society. Foreigners, what foreigners there were left—mostly diplomats and journalists—and those in power, in this case the Maladif junta, congregated around the mahogany tables or at the marble-topped bar of the Excelsior's lounge. They drank champagne and expensive Scotch, and sat down to imported steak dinners, all the while trading rumours, which were the basis for political discourse on the island. In the evenings they were entertained by a local *chanteuse*, a startlingly beautiful young woman with ice-blue eyes and skin the colour of warm mocha. Between sets she sat with a rather fat, middle-aged general who was in charge of military intelligence. When the Marais junta was in power, she'd sat with a different fat general.

I was contemplating all of this while Mathieu eased us down the Avenue-de-la-Mer and away from the hotel. While it was true that the Excelsior was not what I'd hope for, there was, behind its tired pink façade, more romance than I could have ever imagined. Even Marlowe, sick in his bed, the mosquito netting hanging down from the canopy, the fever of a tropical illness shivering his weakening body, enlivened my fantasy.

I turned back round in my seat and looked out at the road ahead. It was crowded with peasants, most of them ragged and spectral, come to the capital city from the surrounding countryside in search of something better. Many pulled handcarts that were piled high with batons of charcoal, or balanced on their heads wicker baskets filled with dried fish and shrivelled plantains, the staple of their meagre diet. Some bore upon their backs the precious sacks of flour and rice donated by the myriad aid agencies that were trying to combat the rampant hunger that plagued the population. In each instance, these individuals were surrounded by a protective phalanx of men carrying crude, heavy-ended clubs, ready to rain blows down upon anyone who might attempt to pilfer the already-pilfered spoils.

So caught up was I by this sorry panorama that I did not hear Mathieu when he spoke to me. He had to reach across and tap me on the shoulder to get my attention.

"*Docteur?*" he said, his eyes bright with alarm in his dark face. "You not well, *Docteur?*"

I followed his gaze as he looked down at my hand, the same hand that Marlowe had taken hold of just a few hours earlier.

"*C'est malaria?*" he said, sounding genuinely concerned.

Communication with Mathieu was difficult. Unlike Marlowe, I could not understand the Creole indigenous to the island and possessed only a paltry French vocabulary. So it came down to Mathieu's limited English and my ability to translate the rest. This last question, however, had been quite simple.

"No," I said, shaking my head. "No. Not malaria. I am fine."

The tremor in my left hand was a sad irony. One lost on neither Marlowe nor myself. After years of exhaustive case studies, experimentation, animal testing, clinical trials, re-evaluations of data, more clinical trials, natural compounds, synthetic cocktails, amalgams of the two, we still had not found anything definitive; indeed, we often ended up with more questions than answers. Then one day I found myself, almost as if by dint of prolonged exposure, in the first stages of the neurological disease we'd been working so hard to combat. The Devil had worked himself within.

My symptoms had not progressed yet beyond the slight tremor in my left hand, though it had been present long enough that I rarely noticed when it occurred. I did my best to deflect notice of this defect by holding my hand close to my body, or carrying in it something heavy enough to mask the shaking. Knowing the disease as I did, I was aware that it wouldn't be long before concealment became impossible. Soon it would affect the whole of my musculature: either the palsy would spread or I would find myself trapped within the rigid clutches of my own body. Either way, I knew my time for finding an answer was quickly running out. But if Marlowe was to be believed, and I could see no reason why he shouldn't, that answer lay in Ascension.

———⟊———

The highway leading away from Cap Gloire was in much better shape than I had expected, especially after the pitiful conditions of the roadways in the capital. It was a two-lane blacktop that stretched with Roman straightness from Cap Gloire to Port Amitié, the country's second city on the northern coast of the island. Before reaching Port Amitié, the highway cut through the Maladif district and the foothills below Ascension. We were to stop there and spend the night in a hotel in the town of Espérance. This was Mathieu's hometown, and I could tell that he was excited at the prospect of spending the evening among friends. In the morning, we would begin our ascent into the mountains. The first leg of our journey would be made on mule-back. The remainder would be on foot through the jungle.

But Espérance was still hours away, and as Mathieu and I were unable to carry on any real sort of conversation, I turned my eyes to the countryside we passed through. At one time, the forest would have encroached upon the highway, muscling in, trying to reclaim the swath that had been cut from its heart. But now the land fell away dry and flat from the verges, taking on the aspect of a poor man's savannah. Far off the road to the east, I could see a struggling copse of native eucalypts trying to establish themselves among the burnt grasses. They would not last long. The next band of migrating peasants to catch sight of them would have the trees cut down and baked into charcoal before their sap had the chance to run dry. I was struck by the resonance this held for the country itself. It was a scene similar to the one that had played itself out innumerable times on this sad island, first by the French, who annihilated the native Indian population, then by the African slaves, who rose up and slaughtered their French masters. And for the past one hundred and fifty years it had been a succession of corrupt regimes, one cutting down another, ensuring that they in turn would be cut down by the next. This was a nation built on shifting, blood-soaked soil. That it was now prepared to offer up something of benefit seemed to me at odds with its cruel legacy. But Marlowe was convinced.

The exuberance he displayed when he telephoned the institute had been infectious. Marlowe rarely made contact when he was in the field. When he did, it was never to discuss the expedition, but usually to plead for more funds. I remember that I was performing the euthanasia of a rhesus monkey in order to take a cross-section of its *substantia nigra*. I had just injected the animal when my assistant called me to the telephone. At first I did not recognize Marlowe's voice. It was ragged with enthusiasm, and on top of that the connection was faulty: there was a delay on the line, as well as an annoying echo.

"For God's sake, James," Marlowe finally said, fed up with my constant interruptions. "Will you just be silent a moment and listen to me. I've found it, James. I have found it."

I admit that initially I was skeptical. Marlowe had made such claims before, most notably on his return from Peru three years before. There he had located a river tribe that dipped the points of its hunting darts into a paste derived from several rare local moulds. A single prick was sufficient to bring down a fully grown wild boar. The animal, once stuck, became completely flaccid, allowing the hunters to safely bleed it while its heart continued to beat. Our hopes had run high, but it became apparent as soon as we began laboratory testing that the agent, rather than effecting the levels of either dopamine or acetylcholine in the brain, was little more than a powerful psychotropic that left its victim trapped in a hallucinogenic void. But there was an edge in Marlowe's voice that told me this new find was different.

"What is it?" I asked him, tucking my shuddering left hand beneath my thigh. "Where is it?"

"It's here, James," Marlowe said, his voice crackling along with the poor connection. "Here on the island. Where I thought it would be. The stories I heard about it were true."

The stories to which Marlowe referred were of a remote jungle village, whose inhabitants, fiercely protective of their own, had managed to cut themselves off from the outside world; in a country where towns and villages were routinely and brutally punished for real or imagined loyalties, such seclusion was exceptional. It had been achieved through sheer reputation: the people of Ascension, it was said, were more cruel, more brutal, than even the most ruthless of the country's regimes. They were also, it was believed, cursed.

"So, it's the voudoun drug that you've been looking for, then?" I said to him. There was a long silence and for a moment I thought we'd been disconnected. Then finally Marlowe spoke: "A rather dramatic term for it, but yes."

I was rehashing our conversation in my mind when, far off in the distance, I saw the dark mountains of the Maladif district, looming like a great bruise on the horizon. The sky above us was an empty, dry blue. I found it strange that this island, though it lay so squarely in the tropics, was enveloped by an arid, almost desert-like heat, as if it were a bone stripped clean and left to crack in the sun. Then I noticed that the sky above the distant hills, while still empty of clouds, displayed a far deeper tinge, as if maybe it contained a different heaven than the one above us.

"Soon, *Docteur*," Mathieu said, his eyes not straying from the road ahead. "Soon Espérance."

We did not see another vehicle until we'd left the highway and started down the rutted dirt road that led to Espérance. About a mile outside the town, we were approached by two military transports. Mathieu had to pull the Land Rover into a shallow gully to let them pass. The beds were crowded with soldiers, their black faces slick with sweat under their heavy, camouflaged helmets. They sat on benches with their rifles propped between their legs. It appeared as if many of them were asleep, their drooping heads lolling back and forth as the trucks bumped and shuddered along the uneven road. I looked at Mathieu. He stared straight ahead as if the passing convoy did not exist, but I could see the worry on his face. We discovered later that the execution of a local government official had taken place that morning. The troops were present to discourage any thoughts of civil unrest. But the people of Espérance knew better than to protest any dictate of the junta. As the desk clerk at the hotel put it: "What is the worth of one man against that of many?"

Mathieu helped me to carry the equipment from the Land Rover to my room on the upper floor of the hotel, then he joined me for dinner in the small bar off the lobby. We ate paella and drank hibiscus tea, followed by several bottles of the local beer, which tasted faintly of formaldehyde. At one point, Mathieu leaned across the table and said to me, in a hushed voice: "Not before. They not let me in. *J'ai grigou.*" I reached out and took hold of his arm. "Not any more," I said, then added in my best French: "*Tu est un homme de science.*" He liked that very much and we raised our glasses to one another. I had begun to regret my initial judgment of this man and thought if only we'd shared a common language we might have possibly become friends.

Mathieu left me after dinner to spend the evening with relatives. I retired, slightly drunk, to my room on the second floor. The hotel, rather ambitiously called La Majesté, was a world away from the Excelsior, even in the latter's present dishevelled state. The colonial facade of La Majesté concealed a rough-hewn interior of creaking floors and paper-thin walls. There was no bath in my room, and the toilets—dark, foul-smelling affairs—were at the far end of the corridor. A single light, suspended beneath a slow-moving ceiling fan, offered the only illumination to my otherwise murky apartment. When I switched it on, several bright green geckos scurried across the dingy papered walls. The bed, when I lay upon it, revealed a great rift running down its middle. And I was almost certain that I felt something moving beneath the sheets. Disconcerted, I pulled myself out of the hollow and set about preparing the equipment for the next day's trek.

The gear I was to take was minimal. Two canteens that I had filled with distilled water before leaving Cap Gloire. A survival kit that included such generic medical supplies as surgical gauze, filament, salt tablets, painkillers, insect repellant, plasters, tensor bandages, peroxide and iodine. There was also a web belt from which hung a very dangerous-looking machete and an airtight, stainless-steel specimen container.

It was the machete that most impressed me. I carefully withdrew it from its long leather sheath and held it up to the light. The newly sharpened edge shone silver. I swung it about me like a sword, imagining that I could hear it cutting the air. I liked the feeling it gave me, and for a moment considered testing the blade on one of the geckos that clung to the wall behind the bed. I decided against this on account of the mess it would cause, though there were several stains on the mouldy wallpaper that hinted at many such eviscerations in the past. Instead, I returned the machete to its scabbard and lay down again on the sway-backed mattress.

Lying there, looking up at the lethargic fan blades, I had an almost desperate urge to speak to Marlowe, to thank him for my being in this place. Of course, there was no telephone in the room; I wasn't certain that there was one in the entire hotel. Besides, it had grown late, and as sick as he was, Marlowe was probably already asleep under his mosquito netting.

It had come as something of a surprise to me when he invited me along. At first, I thought it had been done out of simple politeness, a gesture in recognition of the years we had served together at the institute. During that time we had been amiable, but there was always a slight distance between us. Marlowe was insistent, though, saying that he wanted me to share in the event. I suspected that this persistence was in sympathy of my condition, and I rather admired the sentiment. I was only sorry that now his own illness, impermanent as it was, would keep him from participating in the final stage of our adventure.

—⟋⟋⟋—

Mathieu showed up at the hotel an hour late the following morning, his eyes still yellow with drink. I was waiting for him in the bar, wearing my khaki safari suit, machete-heavy web belt, backpack and Australian bush hat with corks dangling from its wide brim. I was concerned about insects. Needless to say, I received some strange looks from those around me. A few remarks were passed amongst the hotel staff, but as I didn't understand the language, I was not bothered. I think the presence of the machete strapped to my leg curtailed any overt comments.

When Mathieu did finally arrive, the expression on his face caused me some concern. He was drawn and nervous. I was certain, regardless of whatever threats Marlowe may have made, that he was going to back out, was going to manufacture some excuse and send me on my way alone. But he did not. He simply nodded in my direction and waited for me to join him in the lobby. He did not remark upon my attire.

I don't know which was more skittish, the mules or Mathieu. We collected them from an odd little livery on the edge of town. It was no more than a corrugated-iron lean-to with a small corral in front. The transaction was completed without the exchange of a single word. Mathieu strolled across the paddock to where the proprietor, an elderly man whose ebony complexion was deepened by a shock of white hair, sat waiting on an overturned fruit crate. Mathieu handed the man a small crumpled wad of bills, then returned trailing two mules behind him. They were both ragged, stinking beasts, with matted hides and flanks callused by whips. Mathieu

swung his leg over the back of one and motioned for me to do
the same. Sitting atop the animal with my feet barely off the
ground, I felt more than a little foolish as we started on our
way.

The mule leg of the journey took the better part of four
hours, and followed a lazily slow ascent along a winding trail
that repeatedly doubled back on itself. It was as if whoever had
originally beaten the path sought to prolong his inevitable
penetration of the jungle above. The grade of the climb was so
slight that it seemed to me rather pointless that we'd bothered
with the mules at all. The journey could have quite easily
been made on foot, and probably at a quicker pace. I had to
assume that the purpose of the animals was to conserve our
energy for the trek through the forest. I thought to ask this of
Mathieu, but he'd not spoken a word to me since we'd gathered the mules.

It did not take long before the heat became oppressive. The
foothills were sparsely treed, and the sun beat down on us as if
through a magnifying glass. It bore unmercifully upon my
crown, and my hat, whose bobbles I now cursed, grew heavy
with sweat. When the trail came to an end at last, in an
abrupt halt in a narrow clearing, I took the hat from my head
and tossed it into the grass. Mathieu dismounted his mule and
walked over to where the hat lay. He picked it up and, with a
quick swipe of his hand, tore free all the corks from its brim.
Then he handed it back to me, turned and started toward the
edge of the forest.

I slipped down from my mule and very nearly fell to the
ground in pain. It was as if someone had taken a hammer to
my tailbone. I waited, hands on my knees, for the discomfort

to pass. Only after I'd stretched out my back was I certain that the affliction was temporary. Ahead of me, Mathieu waited, his hands on his hips, his expression unsympathetic.

"What about the mules?" I asked him.

He shrugged his shoulders. "They will die," he said.

I glanced back at the stupid beasts, standing near to one another, oblivious to everything, even the flies that clustered about their rheumy eyes.

"But what about their owner?"

Mathieu looked at me.

"We own," he said, then turned and disappeared into the jungle.

—⁓—

It was the smell that struck me first: putrescent, mordant, distinctly fecal. The air so thick with humidity that it felt as if it were leaving a residue in the lungs. And there was no refuge from the stink; the pungency seemed only to intensify as we climbed. The ground beneath our feet absorbed our steps as if we were walking on foam rubber. And from all around us came the sounds of alarmed movement—from the canopy above and the humus below. Birds, monkeys, reptiles, insects. But we saw nothing. We were surrounded by invisible life. Seen, but unable to see.

It was dim in the forest, and our headway was slow. It was not the straightforward incline I had expected. Time and again, after we'd been climbing through steep, unsteady terrain, the ground would fall away and we were forced to descend into a crevasse, only to be faced with an even steeper climb on the other side. My hands grew raw from clutching at branches and roots, and the sharp, rocky outcroppings that speckled the hillside. My thighs burned from exertion, and my lower back went numb. My khaki shirt was soaked through with sweat, as was the waistband of my trousers. The backpack sat between my shoulders like a stone, but my hat, sodden as it was, kept the perspiration from stinging my eyes.

In time we came upon a dense, tangled wall of vines that halted our progress. I was glad at the chance to stop and catch my breath. I watched as Mathieu took his own machete, which he carried in a sling across his back, and began to hack away at the vines. Thinking I might help, I withdrew my own machete. But Mathieu turned quickly around, his long knife extended toward me.

"No," he said, his voice flat and dry. Then he pointed his rusty blade at the canteen hooked on my belt. "Drink," he said.

The water was warm and tasted of plastic, but I swallowed it greedily. I had not realized how thirsty I was until then, though with the amount I had perspired it only made sense that I was dehydrated. As I replaced the cap on the canteen I noticed that the palsy in my hand had grown worse. I'd left my medication back at the hotel. It was of little use to me now, since my symptoms had all but become immune to its effect. With the water settling in my belly, I was overcome by weariness. I wanted nothing more than to sit and rest.

Mathieu had already cut a tunnel a metre deep into the bank of vines and I had to call his name twice before he acknowledged me.

"We'll stop here a while," I said, struggling to give my voice some authority. "Rest our legs."

There was anger in Mathieu's eyes when he regarded me.

"No," he said bitterly, then looked up into the trees. "Dark soon."

I had not even noticed the lengthening of the shadows around us, and when I gazed up into the canopy, I could see through the gaps in the leaves that the sky had begun to deepen toward night.

"How much farther?" I asked.

"Close," Mathieu answered in a hollow tone. "They watch."

His words sent a chill coursing through my body. It was only then that I noticed how quiet the forest had become.

They appeared as if from the darkness itself. Four men standing side by side on a ridge above us. In their hands they carried blunt clubs, like those I'd seen on the Avenue-de-la-Mer. Mathieu saw the men first. We had cut our way through the wall of vines and were starting upward again. When he stopped, I nearly walked into the back of him in the failing light.

The men did not move, but waited for our approach. We climbed slowly, and with each step I fought the urge to flee. Where could I have gone but down, and how long would it have taken them to catch me up? Besides, who was to say that there weren't others waiting in the trees below. Mathieu, for his part, betrayed no sign of alarm. Rather, it seemed as if the tension that had gripped his body the whole day had dissipated. His arms swung loosely at his sides, his shoulders relaxed, his gait became casual.

The men turned away before we gained the ridge. Once we reached the crest, I saw them standing a short distance away, waiting for us to follow. They led us along a path that seemed to simply open up before them: a hole in the foliage that even in the clear light of day would have been obvious only to those aware of its existence. In the grimy twilight I could see no farther than the man directly in front of me, but he did not appear at all devilish. He was slight in build, almost femininely narrow through the shoulders, and wore ragged khaki trousers, the loose-fitting cotton blouse common among the peasant class and a wide-brimmed straw hat. His bare feet made a faint slapping sound as he moved across the moist ground. In all aspects he appeared inconsequential, and I began to wonder if the frightening tales about the villagers of Ascension were not just the product of ignorance. After all, they had not harmed Marlowe on his journey here.

I caught wind of the village before I actually saw it. The familiar aroma of burning charcoal, still the chief cooking fuel used on the island. When Ascension appeared, it did so in the same manner as the four men and their hidden path: as if from the very ether. The village was quite literally cut from the jungle. Situated on a narrow plateau, it consisted of thirty-odd squalid adobe huts, each with a corrugated-iron roof, and was hemmed in on all sides by the great, dark walls of the jungle.

We stopped on the edge of the village, and what I saw before me lightened my heart. It was a picture of community I'd not yet witnessed on the island. Around the open cooking fires, which perfumed the air now with the scent of frying plantain and papaya, women in richly coloured cloth headdresses idly chatted while tending to the flames. And children, unafraid of the coming night, ran carefree between the huts, chasing one another and laughing loudly. On the far side of the village a group of men were gathered beside the wall of a hut, playing a game whose object I could not divine. A cheer rose from their midst, after which handshakes were exchanged. Apparently, no one was bothered by our presence.

I turned to Mathieu, wanting to tell him that all his worry had been for naught, but the look on his face stopped me cold. There was a fear in his eyes so acute, so consuming and so seemingly at odds with our surroundings that I began to shiver. Mathieu offered no resistance as the slender man in the straw hat stepped forward and relieved him of his machete. Then another of the men, one I'd not taken much notice of until then, tall, with a thick neck and dead eyes, stepped toward me.

I watched, as if merely a bystander, as he raised his club high into the air and brought it down fiercely upon my head.

—⟋⟍—

"He really oughtn't to have hit you so hard."

It was Marlowe's voice that brought me round. I could see sunlight through the door of the hut. I was laid out on a straw mat, felt the cool, earthen floor beneath me. My head hurt a great deal, and I was nauseated. There was something sticky in my hair. Then a cold cloth was pressed against my forehead and I heard Marlowe's voice again.

"I've dealt with the man that struck you," he said. "He's been properly punished, though I don't think he meant you any real harm. Still, what's done is done."

It was dark inside the hut, and the air smelled foul. I must have made a face, because Marlowe said, "I'm afraid that's down to you, James. You made quite a mess of yourself last night. I'll have one of the women wash out your trousers."

After he spoke, I could feel someone tugging at my pant legs. I was having difficulty focusing. Marlowe sat on a low stool to my left, but I could make out no more of him than his shape. He was tipped slightly forward. My lips felt dry and cracked, and it took me a moment to find my voice.

"Mathieu," I managed. "Where is Mathieu?"

"I'm afraid he's gone," Marlowe said, leaning back.

"To Espérance?" I asked, and tried to raise myself on my elbows. But even this insignificant movement inflamed the pounding in my head and I had to lie back down. I heard Marlowe chuckle.

"No," he said. "Unfortunately, not."

Where, then? I wanted to ask. If not Espérance, where? But the words wouldn't come, and soon everything began to slip away again.

— ∽ —

When I next awoke it was to an empty hut. The sun was still shining outside, and the pain in my head had subsided enough that I could raise myself from the mat. I surveyed my surroundings, which were Spartan. Except for the tacking on which I lay and the crude stool Marlowe had occupied, there was nothing, just mud walls, a dirt floor and me. It was more like a cell than a domicile.

My nausea had passed and I was wearing my trousers again. I put my hand to my head. There was an angry lump just above my right ear, and the hair around it was brittle with what I assumed to be dried blood.

A shadow fell across me then, as a figure entered the doorway. It stood silhouetted by the sun's brightness, arms akimbo.

"Well, at long last," Marlowe said, and stepped inside. "You had me worried there for a while."

He did not sit down, but rather stood studying me from above, as one might a strange carcass found along the roadside.

"How long?" I asked, rubbing my stiff neck.

"Almost twenty-four hours," he smiled. "You know, it was quite rude to nod off in the middle of a conversation like you did."

"I think I have a concussion."

"Oh, I should think so," Marlowe said, and turned back to the door.

Only then did his presence strike me as odd.

"But you're ill," I said. "The doctor."

He looked back at me, grinning still. "Yes, indeed, James. Quite ill. In fact, I'm under round-the-clock medical supervision. Or so the staff at the Excelsior believes. The virus has progressed to the point where my very life is in danger. On no account am I to be disturbed. All necessary fallacy, I'm afraid."

"Necessary?" I said, not following him. "Necessary why? What are you talking about?"

"You'll see," he said, holding his hand out toward me and crooking his finger. "Let's go. On your feet, James. I think you've lollygagged long enough."

I had to shield my eyes against the sun when I stepped out of the hut. It took a few moments before they adjusted to the glare. When they did, I noticed that a change had come over the village. Gone was the carefree tenor that I'd witnessed on my arrival; in its place, a discernible tension. As I walked along behind Marlowe, I was aware of eyes upon us. The women, so insouciant and oblivious to my presence before, now regarded me with apprehension. Their children they kept close by their sides. The men, too, looked on; their hooded eyes, though, were fixed not upon me, but Marlowe.

As we neared the centre of the village, which was marked by an open space with an awkward rock cairn in its middle, I grabbed hold of Marlowe's elbow. When I did this, I sensed movement off to my left. Marlowe held up his hand, as if in signal.

"Mathieu," I said to him. "Before you told me something about Mathieu. Has he left?"

He looked at me as if I was becoming something of a nuisance.

"In a manner of speaking, James," he said, "yes, he has left."

"What does that mean?" I demanded. "A manner of speaking?"

To see him, one could imagine Marlowe a stern school-master in the process of explaining simple arithmetic to a dim-witted pupil. His arms were crossed over his chest, and his chin dipped toward his collar.

"It is one of the peculiarities of this country," he said, "that people often go missing and yet are rarely missed. As will be the case with our poor Mathieu. His family, what family he has, will no doubt assume the worst. And they will, of course, be correct in their assumption. But they won't bother to look for him, which is a good thing. Seeing as there's not much left to be found."

It was the way in which these words were spoken as much as the words themselves that shocked me: the utter completeness of Marlowe's indifference.

"My God, Marlowe," I said. "What have you done?"

He offered no answer, simply shrugged his shoulders and turned away.

I could not move. The nausea returned. And for a moment, it felt as if the palsy in my hand was about to envelop my entire body. I caught up to Marlowe on the opposite side of the cairn, but my mind was awhirl. I knew I had to say something, but my brain, whether still addled by the blow or simply numb from the revelation, was unable to form the words.

Marlowe, however, suffered no such loss.

"These people," he said laconically, gesturing to the villagers, who watched us from a safe distance. "These people really are quite uncivilized. Oh, I know that's not the *correct* thing to say nowadays, but it's true. Of course, they are by no means the barbarians that the people below think them. Actually, they are a rather peaceful lot. True, they were in the past rather brutal, but it was purely a matter of necessity. They've no *real* taste for violence."

He stopped then, and a broad smile creased his face.

"Not like these fellows," he said, and nodded toward two men leaning against the shaded wall of one of the adobe huts. I immediately recognized their tight-fitting navy jumpsuits and gold epaulettes. They were agents of the *Force Sûreté*.

"What's going on, Marlowe?" I said, understanding now the veil of fear that had descended upon the village. "Why have you brought me here?"

The laugh that issued from his lips was hideous; it sounded as if it were born in the very depths of darkness.

"My dear James," he said, taking my face in his hands. "Have you not figured it out yet? Who better than you, my very own little lab rat."

I did not fight them. I could see no reason to. They were younger; they were stronger. They were the sort of men who feasted on violence. Struggle would have only whetted their appetite. Still, the smaller of the two, a compact, wiry man with the slender fingers of a pianist, could not resist the craving and slapped me hard across the face with the back of his hand. But Marlowe put a stop to any further beating with a few soft words, spoken in Creole.

As they tied me to a straight-backed wooden chair retrieved from one of the huts, I studied their faces. Both were scarred. The man who slapped me had a long angry welt that ran from his hairline down across his cheek. It was raised up and pink. It must have been a very deep cut, and recent. Both men wore mirrored sunglasses, and I wondered why it was that such thugs always thought it necessary to shield their eyes.

When I was tightly bound to the chair, Marlowe had them carry me back to the centre of the village and set me down in front of the cairn. I was put on display for all to see, but the villagers had retreated into their huts, leaving the four of us alone under the blazing sun. One of the agents fetched Marlowe his stool, and he sat down before me.

"So, James," he said, taking hold of my left hand and caressing it in his own, "where is your Sinemet and Eldepryl? I searched your backpack and your pockets but found nothing."

"It's back at the hotel in Espérance," I said.

This pleased him. "Good," he said. "Good. I'd thought of relieving you of your medication in Cap Gloire, but didn't want to raise suspicion. Besides, I could tell by your palsy that wearing-off had already begun. Now, when was your last dosage?"

"I haven't taken anything since we arrived."

Marlowe smiled: "Even better. It will all be out of your system, then. We can get started right away."

I realized now that I did not know this man, that I had never known him. All those years we'd worked together, me acting as his go-between with the bureaucrats at the institute, making certain he had what he needed to continue his search, our search, meant nothing. He paid me for my services with his tales of adventure, maybe the whole while planting the seed that brought me to this God-forsaken place.

"Tell me, Marlowe," I asked, already knowing what the answer would be. "Is there even a drug here?"

"But, of course, James," he laughed. "You don't think I'd have gone through this ridiculous charade if there wasn't, do you? What a silly question."

"How about the pharmaceutical companies?" I said. "The ones who are greasing the palms, as they say?"

"Now that, I'll admit, was something of an exaggeration. But mark my words, James. There *will* be pharmaceutical companies. And their pockets will be very deep indeed."

"So that's what this is all about, then," I said.

Marlowe scrunched up his face and gave me a look of mock disapproval, then waggled his finger.

"I'm surprised at you, James. You know as well as I that it's always about that."

He turned away from me then and spoke to the smaller man, who then went to the nearest hut, returning a moment later with a leather satchel. Marlowe took the bag and sat it between his feet.

"You know, it really is quite a fascinating narcotic," he said, as he withdrew a hypodermic syringe and a glass phial. "At first I thought it to be a variation on the more common voudoun drug used in rituals all across the island. But it is, in fact, an altogether different beast. You see, the others employ a laughably rudimentary concoction of mescaline and ergotised grass seed, while these clever buggers have found themselves a nasty little tree frog whose skin exudes, would you believe it, a wholly unique form of tetrodotoxin."

Marlowe smiled and held the phial out before him; the grin on his face was that of a small boy who has just found a shiny stone.

"All quite exciting, really," he said. "Who knows, if we play our cards right, we may even be able to set up a little gourmet concern on the side. Could be big with the Japanese. We could import a gaggle of *fugu* chefs to the Excelsior and offer up a double course of pufferfish and Maladif *grenouilles*. Of course, we would have to take great care with the recipe."

Marlowe seemed to be finding all of this quite funny, and when he laughed, the *Force Sûreté* men laughed with him, though I doubt they understood a single word he said.

"Now these heathens," Marlowe went on, motioning toward the surrounding huts, "use the drug in its powder form. They blow it into the intended's face, so that it is inhaled and absorbed through the mucous membrane. Or else they mix it with crushed nettles and spread it over the ground. The small lesions produced are sufficient to allow the drug into the bloodstream. Both remarkably inefficient delivery systems, if you ask me. Injection is far more expeditious."

He pushed the needle through the rubber stopper in the phial and began to extract the plunger.

"Shall I tell what makes this wee potion so remarkable, James?" He waited for me to answer, and when I didn't, he looked mildly perturbed. "You do have the right to know."

Again he waited. I said nothing.

"Don't be petulant, James," Marlowe sneered. "It doesn't become you." He held the loaded syringe at arm's length and depressed the plunger so that a stream of the solution shot into the air.

"Fine," I said. "Why don't you tell me what's so remark-able."

"Gladly, James. Gladly." His smirk returned. "Unlike the primitive concoction they employ down below, or indeed the *chiri* favoured by Nipponese gourmands," Marlowe said, "this lovely little wonder does not affect heart rate nor, I'm pleased to say, does it depress respiration. This is no bogeyman potion, James. No Baron Samedi trick to steal the soul. In fact, for all its artlessness, it is quite sophisticated. Very specific. It seems to work exclusively on the voluntary musculature, inducing complete paralysis. There's many an inmate in Cap Gloire's central prison that could attest to that. Well, at least

they could have," he said, casting a sly glance toward the two
Force Sûreté men, "had my friends here not paid them a visit in
the infirmary."

"And me?" I asked. "Why me?"

"Please, James," he said, shaking his head. "I should have
thought it obvious by now. You are the perfect choice. Not
only do you have a thorough professional knowledge of the
disease, but you are also its victim. What more could a scientist ask for than a subject that can report on the effects from
both the inside and out?"

I took a deep breath and thought that maybe it would have
been better if I had put up a fight. Then I wondered about
Mathieu. I wondered if he had fought. Or did he let them take
his life as easily as they did his machete?

"This is madness," I said. "You know that, don't you?"

"On the contrary, James. I see it as pure science."

"And what about afterward? After you've catalogued your
findings. What then?"

Marlowe pursed his lips and looked down at the ground.

"You went into the Maladif jungle with a local guide in
search of a community well known for being hostile to
outsiders. Neither you nor your guide was ever seen again. It
was only by the grace of God and a nasty little viral infection
that I didn't suffer the same fate."

"And that's it?" I said.

"Yes, James," Marlowe replied. "That's it."

He motioned to one of the men, who retrieved a bottle of
rubbing alcohol and a ball of cotton batting from the satchel.
Marlowe held the syringe between his teeth as he swabbed the
crook of my left arm.

It took only seconds for the drug to start taking effect. I recognized in myself the initial signs of tetrodotoxin poisoning, almost as if I were witnessing them in a lab specimen. My motor coordination began to fail and the entire surface of my skin was soon numb. I began to salivate; a long string of spittle slipped from the corner of my mouth and hung, unbroken, from my chin. I could feel my muscles weaken and my head started to droop. The sensation was quite frightening at first. It felt as if tiny strings throughout my body were unravelling, as if I were coming undone. There was a flash of heat behind my eyes. From there it radiated out and I was bathed in warmth, from the top of my skull to the tips of my toes. This was followed by a pleasant sense of hollowness, as if I'd been emptied out, leaving just the shell of me, nothing else.

I could hear Marlowe's voice, coming at me as if over a great distance. It wavered, then was loud again, as if it were being tossed about by the wind.

"James," I heard him call. "Are you still with us, James?" He lifted my head and peered into my eyes. "Of course you are," he said. "You're still in there."

He was grinning like a cat.

"Don't you forget, James," he said, almost shouting now. "Don't you forget what it feels like. Notes; a good scientist always takes notes. Now," he said, gently turning my head to the side, "have a look at this."

He was showing me my hand, my left hand. It lay motionless on my thigh. As still as it had been in many months, not a tremor to be seen. As if my body were at last my own again.

Then Marlowe turned my face back toward his own, and I noticed in it a look akin to compassion.

"I think that's good enough for our first go-round, don't you?" He nodded my head for me. "I'm going to give you another shot now, James," he said, as if he was explaining a simple medical procedure to a worried child. "It's a mild *Datura stramonium* derivative. Has some rather intriguing hallucinogenic properties, but nothing too potent."

At this point, Marlowe motioned to one of the others to hold my head while he prepared a second syringe. He administered it very near the puncture mark left by the first. Then he stepped back and waited, looking more than satisfied with himself. But when nothing happened, his demeanour changed. He became agitated.

He waited a moment longer, then knelt down on the ground in front of me and put his hands on my shoulders.

"James," he said in a ridiculously stern voice. "Are you listening to me, James? I'll have no games here. This is serious business."

The *Force Sûreté* man holding me from behind spoke. I did not understand what he said, but his tone was distinctly unfriendly. Marlowe hissed at him in indecipherable Creole, then reached for his satchel and withdrew another syringe.

"One more, James," he said, offering me a hopeful look. "But that's it. I don't want you bouncing around this place like a madman."

Thirty minutes later, I still showed no signs of re-emerging from the stupor. Frustrated, Marlowe grabbed me by my hair and pulled my head back over my shoulders. He put his face very close to mine and shouted my name repeatedly. Small foamy pockets of saliva collected in the corners of his mouth. And as he yelled, the veins in his neck bulged. He could not tell that I was laughing at him.

He ordered the men to cut me loose from the chair. They carried me back to the hut and laid me down again on the straw mat.

—◊◊—

As near as I could tell, the two men from the *Force Sûreté* left before evening fell. Until then, they had remained standing just inside the doorway to the hut, eyeing Marlowe as he worked to revive me. As the hours passed, he grew more frantic.

My third injection of the *Datura stramonium*, though it showed no outward effect, served to produce some rather interesting visions. At one point, I thought I saw Mathieu leaning over me, grinning, and telling me in a voice that sounded much like my own that he had gone back and found the mules, and that he'd returned them safely to the old man's livery. Then Mathieu's face began to swirl about, like water over a drain, until it was gone altogether, replaced by a large black fly buzzing in the air above me.

After the *Force Sûreté* men had left, Marlowe calmed considerably, though he appeared no less concerned about my condition. In their absence, he began to look to more arcane remedies to resuscitate me. He directed the villagers to produce balms and mud packs, and he spread a paste made from tree bark on the inside of my lips and under my tongue. The whole of the while he nattered away, scolding me one moment, the next caressing my brow and whispering softly into my ear. Most of what he had to say did not register, so addled was I by the hallucinogenic cocktail he'd fed into my veins.

For a day and a half he disappeared. I can only assume he went back to Cap Gloire for supplies, because when he returned he brought with him several new intravenous variants of the original *Datura stramonium* derivative, each of increased potency. None produced any greater effect than magnifying my apparitions, and further deflating his own spirit. These failures took their toll. When he looked down at me, the disappointment registered in his features. Of the two of us, I'd no doubt that it was I who now appeared the younger. A thought that pleased me greatly.

Then, a few days after Marlowe's return from Cap Gloire, a colonel of the *Force Sûreté* came to the village. He and Marlowe stood outside of the hut arguing, their voices cracking in anger. When they came inside, the officer took out a handkerchief and held it over his nose and mouth. By then, the smell in the hut was ungodly. The sad fact was, with the paralysis of my voluntary musculature, I no longer had the ability to control my bodily functions. And the thin gruel that Marlowe forced down my throat through a feeding tube fashioned out of a length of rubber surgical tubing went through me like Pablum through a newborn. As he refused any assistance from the villagers, the job of my cleaning fell to Marlowe; it was not a duty he performed regularly.

The officer was clearly disgusted by the sight that greeted him. He stared at me for a long moment before he finally bent over and held his hand close to my mouth to see if I was still breathing. He looked familiar, but I couldn't quite place him.

Possibly we had met in the lounge of the Excelsior. Satisfied that I was still alive, he retreated. He said something to Marlowe, then turned and kicked me repeatedly in the upper thigh. When I did not respond, he withdrew his revolver and placed the muzzle against my temple. I heard the click of the hammer being cocked. Marlowe moved forward then and grabbed him by the shoulder, at which the officer spun round on his heels and pressed the barrel against Marlowe's forehead. Then he laughed and re-holstered his weapon. He draped his arm across Marlowe's shoulder and led him outside.

I did not see Marlowe again after that.

Yesterday I heard the sound of fighting. Mortar rounds and small-arms fire. It came from far off, somewhere down below the village. Espérance, I should expect. I could only suppose that officers from some other district on the island had decided it was their time to assume control of this terrible place. Or maybe it was the Marais junta, arisen from the ashes.

Fighting raged throughout the day and there was much commotion in the village. I could hear children crying, women too. The voices of the men were harsh and insistent. The corrugated-steel roofs were being removed from the surrounding huts and dragged across the hard-packed earth. They were placed against the outside walls of my hut, sheet after sheet, and I found the rusty, chiming sound of the panels of metal falling together comforting, as if I were being sealed up in an encrusted cocoon.

As night fell, and the noise of the battle grew closer, the villagers began to flee Ascension, seeking refuge in the jungle higher up in the mountains. But before they left, a small group came into the hut and stripped me of my clothes, as has happened every night since Marlowe disappeared. In his absence they assumed my keeping. It is a responsibility shared among them, and in their hands I have felt a degree of security I could not have previously thought possible. Their kindness, though, is not a gesture of acceptance, for I do not belong here. And yet it is kindness nonetheless. It is no doubt born of pity, and that pity in turn born of compassion. I have seen it in their faces as they lean over me, their wet cloths sliding over my skin, cleansing my body. But there was something else in their eyes on this night, something they tried to keep hidden from me: sadness, regret.

As their faces passed back and forth across my field of vision, I saw among them the features of the thin man I had followed along the darkened path that led me to this place. He knelt on the floor beside me and put his mouth close to my ear. He whispered something in his singsong dialect that I did not understand and softly kissed the spot where the club had struck me. Then he took the wide-brimmed straw hat from his head and placed it gently over my face. The last sound I heard was that of his bare feet gently slapping against the earthen floor as he left my hut.

PAYNE'S FLIGHT

THE MAN WHO OCCUPIED THE WINDOW SEAT insisted on climbing over him to gain the aisle, rather than allowing Payne to get up and let him pass. Twice already he'd made the assault, and he was preparing to do so again. When Payne noticed this he moved quickly, undoing his seat belt and grabbing hold of the headrest in front of him. A polite tap on his elbow stopped him from lifting himself any farther. There ensued a smiling pantomime, the silly dumb show of those who do not speak one another's language. The mummeries of his fellow traveller won out, and Payne settled back uncomfortably. He watched as the man went through his strange pre-clambering routine. In the impossibly narrow gap afforded by their coach-class berth, made only slightly more spacious by the vacancy of the middle seat in their row, the man executed several knee thrusts, like a sprinter warming in the blocks. Then, without a pause, he climbed, gracefully Payne had to admit, onto the empty seat. And after two more knee thrusts, possibly to synchronize his rhythm, he passed over Payne and into the aisle.

A queer little fellow, Payne thought as he turned in his seat and watched the man make his way toward the toilets in the rear of the airplane. He was impeccably dressed in varying shades of charcoal, from his smart pullover down to the felt slippers covering his expensive socks. Japanese, Payne decided as he reached into the seat pocket in front of him and withdrew his spiral notebook. He unclipped his pen from the coils and flipped to the page he had been working on earlier. Before continuing, he reread what was already written:

> Esteemed colleagues—for that is what I consider you,
> both professors and pupils alike. We are all, regardless
> of achievements, confederates, compatriots—compeers,
> if you will. Bound together in our quest, our thirst, by a
> love that is far deeper than simple admiration. It is a
> passion that embraces our souls, that settles in our
> bones, that stirs our loins.

Loins? Payne thought. Stirring? How asinine. To be sure, there had been occasions on which his loins had been stirred, but never by literature; at least not by proper literature. He glanced down to the bottom of the page, to where he had written her name—to where he'd written it, crossed it out, drawn a circle around it and then filled in the circle so all was hidden.

For good measure he put another thick line through the blot of ink, then tore the sheet from his notebook. But instead of crumpling it into a ball, as had been his intention, he folded it neatly and slipped it into the inside pocket of his jacket. Then he stared at the blank page before him. The symposium was set to begin at one o'clock the following afternoon, with his address scheduled to close the first day, at a dinner being held in his honour. And all Payne had was the folded piece of paper in his pocket.

—⟋⟍⟍⟍—

Three months earlier when the invitation had arrived, it was completely unexpected. It wasn't so much that Payne hadn't heard of Hoogeveen Polytechnic, which he hadn't, it was that someone at Hoogeveen Polytechnic had heard of Severn College—and Professor Harvard T. Payne of Severn College in particular. His first reaction was fear, sure as he was that it was just another cruel faculty joke. Only after a rather arduous overseas phone call were his anxieties quelled. "*Ja, Dokter Payne,*" Professor Willem Hefflin, the invitation's signatory, assured him, "we are very excited to have you speak. Your work on Gaynor is well regarded." At that, Payne considered again the possibility of an elaborate jape.

His research on the slim canon of Noel Gaynor, whom Payne believed to be a significant figure in the birth of Canadian letters—at least as important, if not more so, than those uptight émigré sisters, Moodie and Traill—was considered by his fellow professors at Severn to be something of an embarrassment. After Payne's seminal work on the subject, a slim article entitled "Noel Gaynor: Lost in the Bush," had been turned down by all the respectable academic journals, he'd finally had to subsidize its publication in an obscure periodical put out by a West Coast university even more insignificant than Severn. Many within his own English department held the view that his tenure was the result of an administrative oversight. A clerical error, Payne had overheard one colleague say. Thus, the invite to the symposium was indeed a coup. One that Payne was more than prepared to flaunt. With it also came the promise of adventure. The thought of a stopover in Amsterdam with Kathryn made him tingle.

Payne called her after verifying the invitation's authenticity. He'd settled himself down behind his cluttered desk in his cramped little office, which was tucked away in the farthest reaches of the Victorian manor that housed the English department. He couldn't be sure, hadn't found any hard evidence, but was fairly certain that the room had once been part of the servants' quarters, situated, as it was, on the top floor of the old house. Wedged under the gable of the roof, its ceiling was crossed with beams that drooped so low at the edges he could stretch to his full height—just slightly under five foot eight—only in the middle of the room. Still, there was the consolation of the view afforded by the dormer window behind his desk, which looked out over the gravel-packed faculty parking lot to the thick copse of sugar maples beyond. The bush, he liked to call it, in deference to his woodsman scribe.

He sat there, his feet resting on the radiator, looking out at the autumnal colours, and dialled the number for Kathryn's cellphone. Payne experienced a slight twinge of desire as he waited for the call to go through. Kathryn, if he recalled her timetable, would be in Foden's classics at Wieschuck Hall on the main campus. She would most definitely have switched the ringer to vibrate, so as to avoid the embarrassment of disturbing the lecture. Payne closed his eyes and listened to the tone, trying to picture the phone jiggling against her flesh—Kathryn kept it hooked on her belt loop—and leaning back in his chair, breathed deeply, imagining the sweet scent of the skin below her navel, and the fine downy fluff there that had tickled his nose just a few hours earlier.

"Hello?"

"Koochie-koo, sweetie?"

"Harvey? What are you doing? I'm in the middle of a class here."

She sounded upset, and Payne thought for a moment that he'd made a mistake, that she wouldn't share his excitement.

"I've got some wonderful news," he said, his voice a little too eager.

"Well, what is it?"

He paused. She was clearly in a sour mood.

"This isn't a good time, is it?"

"What do you think?"

"Later, then. Come to my place. I'll make you dinner and tell you then." There was silence on the line. "It really is wonderful," he added.

"Fine, Harvey. Fine. I've got to go. Professor Foden's staring at me."

She hung up without saying goodbye. Payne looked at the telephone in his hand. Yes, a mistake. He should have waited. Kathryn was temperamental at the best of times, and drawing the ire of Gil Foden, who was a genuine tyrant, would set her off to no end. Still, candlelight, gnocchi and a sweet red might bring her back round. And if that didn't, Payne was sure Amsterdam would.

—∿—

The drop-down dinner tray nudged against his belly. The passenger in the seat in front of him insisted on having his seat fully reclined, and Payne decided to suffer the discomfort rather than have to engage in any conversation, no matter how trivial. He looked down at his meal. He had chosen the beef over the fish, having never been partial to seafood. It was meant to be stroganoff, but the limp noodles and minuscule cuts of meat seemed to him insufficient. The dessert, an unidentifiable custard, both in colour and taste, was too airy. And the plastic wrap over his cheese had a hole in it, leaving the contents hard and stale. He enjoyed his wine, though, a nondescript Merlot in a small twist-top bottle. He considered asking the flight attendant for another, but stopped himself. There was no point, he concluded, in muddling his senses when he was going to have to navigate his way through the airport to find the connecting flight to Maastricht, and from there the train to Hoogeveen.

"Are you finished, sir?" The flight attendant stood in the aisle beside him, her hand on the back of his seat, leaning in so that her face was close to his. She had large dark eyes and brown hair cut in a bob, her skin pale, with just the faintest dusting of foundation. "No . . . I mean, yes." Her closeness made Payne anxious, and he could feel his face begin to flush. "Yes, I'm finished, thank you."

"A little more wine, maybe?" she asked, with a smile that revealed a neat row of straight white teeth. Her lips, Payne could see, were moist, as if she had just passed her tongue across them.

"No, thank you. I'm fine, really," he said, and nodded, almost banging his forehead against her chin.

"Very good then," she replied, and lifted the half-finished remnants of his dinner from the tray. Then she reached across and took away his neighbour's platter. Payne closed his eyes as the fabric of her blouse brushed his cheek.

He had noticed early on in the flight that the attendants were, to a one, quite attractive, and it had made him nervous. Payne had always been uncertain around pretty women. He couldn't help but watch them, how they moved, how they reacted to others. What it must be like to be a beautiful person in this world, he often wondered, when there are so many people who simply are not.

His uneasiness was heightened now by the knowledge that these women, in their loose white blouses, their snug navy skirts and vests, and silk neckerchiefs, were Dutch. He'd heard the stories about the Dutch, about their permissiveness. After all, it was this that had so excited him about Amsterdam. As the flight attendant moved on and leaned over to speak to another passenger, Payne stared at her buttocks and contemplated the wondrously indulgent feats she might be willing to perform.

He recalled reading somewhere that at Schiphol Airport there was a brothel lounge, completely legitimate, certified by the government. The idea was to pander to international businessmen who had to pass through, on their way from one stress-filled corporate engagement to another. Briefly Payne considered checking the duration of his layover between flights, but before he could even dig his itinerary from his jacket pocket, misgiving quashed any idea of an assignation.

He'd been right, Kathryn was angry.

"Do you know what it's like?" she said, standing in the doorway of his kitchen, one hand firmly planted on her hip, the other waving a smouldering cigarette accusingly in his direction. "Do you even have an inkling of how it felt to be singled out in the middle of a lecture hall by that man?"

Payne kept his head down and tried to concentrate on the potato dumplings boiling in the pot before him, while at the same time making certain his sauce didn't burn. He needed a few more drops of olive oil in the water to keep the gnocchi from sticking, but to have added it would've simply upset Kathryn further. She'd already accused him of not paying enough attention to her needs.

"I'm sorry," he said, casting a furtive glance toward the doorway.

She let out an exasperated breath and brought the cigarette to her lips. Through a cloud of smoke she said, "You know, Harvey, you can't always be sorry."

Then she turned and walked into the living room, and soon the thumping of the stereo, its volume tuned higher than he would have thought possible, reverberated through the house. Payne had never understood her taste in music: angry, violent, discordant. He'd tried several times to coax her toward his own musical preferences. But she'd turned up her nose at Schubert and Chopin, and when he'd parried with Leonard Cohen, she'd fallen asleep halfway through the first side of the album. In the end he had to admit that it was her disregard for his own notions that attracted him; he was drawn to her wilfulness and occasional contempt. A failing on his part, possibly, but then again, failing was something Payne understood intimately.

The gnocchi, drenched in thick marinara sauce; the bruschetta with the crisply toasted Italian bread, fresh hothouse tomatoes and finely diced onions; the sweet gelato; the perfectly aged Chianti: all had the desired effect. Kathryn, sated, had relaxed considerably. Stretched out on the sofa, eyes closed, her head in Payne's lap, she breathed steadily, edging toward slumber. For his part, Payne had to suppress the urge to belch, not wanting to disturb the moment.

"I'd completely forgotten," she said lazily, opening her eyes to him. "You wanted to tell me something, didn't you?" Then added, mockingly: "Something wonderful."

Payne shifted so that Kathryn had to lift herself into a sitting position, then he put a hand on each of her shoulders. He looked her straight in the eye, and in a voice he hoped would sound both mature and enticing, said, "What is the first thing you think of when I say *Amsterdam?*"

"Anne Frank," Kathryn replied, without missing a beat.

"Oh. Well . . . *Really?*" Payne said, rather at a loss. "Yes, I guess I could see how someone could come up with that. It's not quite what I had in mind."

Payne cleared his throat.

"Let's try it again," he said, and furrowed his brow, as if to imply that Kathryn should concentrate a little harder. "Now, without being so morbid, what's the first thing you think of when I say *Amsterdam?*"

She took a moment longer to answer him the second time: "Canals?"

Payne grimaced.

"Windmills?"

His head drooped.

"Wooden shoes? Rembrandt? Vermeer?" Kathryn pushed his hands away and huffed: "Oh, for God's sake, Harvey. How am I supposed to know what you want me to think?"

Sensing another shift in her mood, toward one that would hardly be conducive to his plans for the remainder of the evening, Payne placed a reassuring hand on her thigh.

"Look, sweetie, I apologize. I shouldn't play games like that."

"I hate games."

"Yes, I know. It's just that . . ." Payne slid a little closer to her. "It's just that I was so excited, I guess I wanted to build up the suspense a bit."

"If you have something to tell me," Kathryn said, straightening herself, "I wish you would just come out and say it."

"Very well." Payne could no longer hide his sly grin. "I've been invited to a symposium in Holland in January and I want you to come with me."

There was a long silence, during which neither of them moved, and Payne could feel his grin begin to wane.

"You want to take me to Holland?" Kathryn said, after what had seemed an eternity. There was little in her tone or expression that gave Payne any reassurance.

"Yes," he said meekly.

"Oh, Harvey!" She threw her arms around him and pulled him so close that for a moment he lost his breath. "Harvey, that's wonderful."

She kissed his cheek and then his ear, taking the lobe between her teeth.

"I thought you might like that," he said, his words now flush with confidence.

"Like it?" she said, her breath warm in his ear. "I think it's amazing."

Then she pushed him roughly away, and Payne fell backward, banging his head on the armrest of the sofa.

"Amsterdam!" she blurted, and then in a low, growling voice, as she crawled toward him: "Oh, Harvey, you naughty little boy, you."

Although he had never really been one for films, Payne had been looking forward to the in-flight movie. The television screens, suspended from the ceiling at ten-foot intervals, had advertised a romantic comedy. He had no doubt that it would be utterly vacuous and implausible, but still Payne had welcomed the thought of a diversion. Unfortunately, it was not to be. A malfunction in the airplane's audiovisual system saw to that. Not only was the film, as well as the news and sports programming, cancelled, but the personal headsets offered nothing beyond static. Payne switched back and forth among the twelve channels on his armrest console and found nothing but white noise.

Looking around, it seemed to him that he was the only one bothered by the situation. The little man beside him was curled neatly against the window, his complimentary blanket tucked under his chin, fast asleep. Payne wished he could sleep, wished he could close his eyes and let the rest of the flight slip by unnoticed. But there was little chance of that. He felt strangely wide awake, fidgety even. And to add insult to injury, in place of the televised entertainment, a map of the airplane's progress was displayed on the screens.

The childlike image of a white aircraft was superimposed over a tract of bright blue labelled *Atlantische Oceaan*. From the tail of the little plane stretched a long red line reaching all the way back to Toronto. Below the crude map was a list of figures: air speed, altitude, elapsed time and time to destination. Looking at the screen, Payne was reminded of the old saying: a watched pot. And for a moment, he could have sworn that he saw the tiny white airplane move backward.

If only that were possible, Payne thought, and imagined flicking a switch on his console that would set everything in reverse, like the rewind button on the tape deck of his stereo. He didn't want to go too far back, just to the departure lounge and his phone call to Kathryn—or maybe two weeks earlier. Yes, two weeks earlier would be better. Then again, if he was honest with himself, a rearward leap of a month would be his best bet to set things straight. A month would allow him to nip the whole thing in the bud, sever the shoot before it even had the chance to bloom.

Just thinking about it was beginning to upset him, to give him an uneasy feeling in his stomach, as if the fruity Merlot were doing battle with the unsavoury stroganoff. So he turned his mind instead to the new lines he'd scribbled after he'd finished eating.

Payne had peppered this new draft of his address with empty appreciation of his Dutch colleagues, as well as mention of a tenuous kinship in the plight of their respective cultures in the face of overwhelming outside influence. It was, he knew, utterly transparent, and would be recognized as not only slapdash but insincere. He no longer cared, however. Everything about this excursion now seemed delusive to him. The thin blankets and flat pillows handed out to the coach passengers as a pretense to comfort, the sinewy strips of beef in his inedible dinner, even the forced pearly smiles arbitrarily dispensed by the comely flight attendants struck Payne as dishonest. The symposium itself, as Gil Foden had so smugly pointed out to him the previous week, was also a sham: the dubious mandate of an equally questionable EU funding scheme.

But most deceitful of all, Payne decided, closing his notebook and putting it to one side, was the empty seat between himself and his slumbering neighbour.

—⚏—

The marijuana they'd smoked in preparation for their excursion to Amsterdam took Payne back to his own student days, but the tales he recounted for Kathryn, while they took the slightly acrid smoke into their lungs, were more fiction than fact. The actualities, which flooded back into his lightened head as the pot began to obstruct his senses, were those of frightened paranoia, unruly limb-twitching tics and the desperate need to belong. He remembered darkened parties in pungent, squalid basement apartments where the incessant permutations of progressive rock LPs replaced conversation and keggers with meaty-fisted frat boys jamming roaches in his face and calling him "faggot" if he declined. Payne mentioned none of this to Kathryn.

He borrowed sexual lore as well. And one night, as he settled his nose between her thighs, he related to her the particulars of an ancient *Playboy* article that had remained with him since his youth. The photograph, a two-page spread that accompanied the text, had burned itself into his inexperienced brain. A tangle of naked bodies—he'd counted twenty-three, always imagining himself the uncommitted extra man—all tongues and teeth and fingertips licking and nibbling and pinching strange nipples and nether parts. Many a night that sybaritic vision warmed the otherwise cold sheets of his bed. Forsaking verity, he performed a quick mathematical function, subtracting twenty gyrating torsos, so that the solution contained only himself and two eager yet unskilled coeds, hungry for tutelage in the more slippery arts.

He harboured no illusions about Kathryn's gullibility: it was doubtful that she believed his tales. Rather, she took from them only what she required. Just as had been the case when she'd sat across the desk from him that first time two semesters before and explained that she would need at least a B+ average in his CanLit 301 to get into the grad school of her choice. She knew what she wanted, and he had it to give. But things had gone on from there, much to Payne's surprise; a pleasant surprise. And soon he found that they each had something the other needed, though he did at times feel that she was after more than he. Especially in the bedroom, where he thought he might be gaining the upper hand, that is until she arched her back and in a breathy voice said, "You know, Harvey, that might be an idea."

"What might be?" he asked, craning his neck, trying to see her face.

"You know," she said languidly.

Payne lifted himself slightly and looked over the slight plumpness of her belly, but her generous breasts, even though somewhat flattened in repose, still hid her from view.

"No," he replied, a quaver coming into his voice. "I don't know that I do."

Kathryn raised herself on her elbows and smiled coquettishly down the length of her bare torso.

"Another body," she said with counterfeit schoolgirl innocence. Then added, with the growl she'd taken to using since he'd told her of the trip: "Why, a little ménage à trois, my darling."

Payne felt his excitement begin to slacken and then go limp, replaced by a flush of panic that was, thankfully, masked by the dimness of the bedroom. He suppressed the urge to ask what gender she had in mind, afraid, either way, of what her answer might be, and instead replied: "Why tinker with a good thing?"

Kathryn laughed and pressed her thighs against the sides of his head so that they covered his ears. Her voice came to him as if he were under water, and Payne had to wriggle free of her grip and ask what she'd said.

"I said, 'You poor dear,'" she repeated, bringing her feet together midway down his back, "'there's always room for improvement.'" And then, flexing her solid calf muscles, she forced him back down to business.

— ∞ —

Payne closed his eyes, not out of tiredness but because with them open he couldn't keep from staring at the television monitors, watching and waiting for another minute, another mile to tick by. He'd abandoned the address, for now at least. There would be time enough to finish it on the train, during that last leg to Hoogeveen. He turned his thoughts instead to Noel Gaynor, to his book, which he was now certain—as certain as he was that he was sitting in a KLM 747M 31,000 feet above the *Atlantische Oceaan*—would never be finished.

He'd brought his notes along, had packed his jottings and the three and a half chapters he'd rushed through in the weeks leading up to the trip, as well as the photocopies of the few unsent letters Gaynor had written to his wife, whom he'd left behind in England when he made his journey to the New World. All was crammed into the attaché case wedged in the overhead compartment.

Of Gaynor's slim volume of abandoned correspondence there were two letters in particular that Payne always found himself coming back to. They were written less than a week apart, and the last just the day before Gaynor disappeared into the dark forests of the Algonquin. These, and others, were found—along with the three brief novellas Gaynor had penned, only two of which survived burning—among his effects at the lumber shanty where he worked as a sawman. The first letter was manic in its composition, in terms of both language and the hectic swirl of the hand; a mind committed and raging:

Penelope,

All is nothing after the wilds. There is no truth, no beauty, in your world. In the world I once shared with you. It evaporates in the face of this wondrous nature I have found. Meanness and meaninglessness is all that

civilization has to offer. The toil and struggle of that
world is for naught, for that is what it makes of a man.
Naught. Knot. Not. The real truth is here. The noth-
ingness of the bush, for that is what they say is out
here: nothing but trees, nothing but beasts, nothing
but savages.

I will not see you again, my wife. I am going away
into the forest never to return. When they ask you, and
they will, what became of your husband, tell them this:
nothing.

Yours, etc.,

N.

Reading it that first time after he'd rescued it, along with
Gaynor's original handwritten manuscripts, from a moulder-
ing packing crate in the bowels of the National Library in
Ottawa, Payne was struck by the perfect nihilism. He was
elated; it was like finally finding the legendary pirate treasure
of Oak Island. And to be sure, when Payne first contemplated
Gaynor for his doctoral dissertation, his subject was as fabulous
as that buccaneer loot. The only mention of him in academic
texts was as a footnote, more often than not in reference to
other writers of the time: Moodie, Traill, Richardson, et al.
And as for his two slim fictions—*The Woodsman of the
Northern Woods* and *The Shaman and the Sawman*—the editions
published by permission of the poor destitute Penelope, in
hope of somehow lessening the privation into which she'd
fallen, they had long ago crumbled into dust.

So when he'd cut loose the stiffened string that had long
bound the crate, and breathed in those first stale spores of

disregard, Payne felt as if he were breathing in a brilliant future rather than a neglected past. His hope soared even higher when he came to the final, unsigned missive:

My Dearest Penelope,
Paradise will be your reward.
As for me—I am at the gates:
Per me si va ne la citta dolente
Per me si va ne l'etterno dolore
Per me si va tra la perduta gente

How quickly all that confidence and hope had dissolved, Payne thought, nestling his head now into the small hollow created by his tilted seat back and the upright back of the empty seat between himself and his snoring companion. It had started to dwindle during his thesis defence.

He'd been so cocksure beforehand, as he sat on the hard wooden bench outside the examination room. But once inside, seated on an equally hard wooden straight-backed chair before his stern-faced inquisitors, he'd felt it all start to slip away. His argument—that Gaynor's nihilism, present both in his letters and his literature, could be viewed as a precursor to the French existentialism that followed some six decades later, because after all, what was an existentialist but a nihilist with an axe to grind?—fell on deaf ears. One of his examiners, a withered old professor with an incongruously dark shock of hair, went so far as to say, "This Gaynor, I wonder if rather than a nihilist, as you seem bent on contending, he simply had nothing to say. For that is the impression I draw from your thesis. But perhaps again, Mister Payne, it is you who are the nihilist."

And there it began, Payne thought, opening his eyes once more to the static blue wash of the television monitors. Dante Alighieri, Noel Gaynor and Harvard T. Payne standing before the gates that lead unto the suffering city, unto eternal pain, unto the way that runs among the lost.

—∿—

Payne couldn't bring himself to rent the video, so Kathryn did. He suggested that maybe they go to a different store, one farther away from his house, but she laughed and made her way into the partitioned adult section and left him standing alone beside a rack of computer games. He wished he'd waited in the car, and was just about to make his way back down the aisle toward the exit when she re-emerged, a wide happy smile curling her lips.

"I think you'll like this," she said, holding up a cassette case that bore the picture of a great buxom blonde with her legs pulled up to her chest and wooden shoes on her feet. "See what it's called," Kathryn smiled: *"Double Dutch."*

The title, as it turned out, was a trifle misleading. For while there were many instances of doubling up in the film, there was little about it that was Dutch. But the incongruity did not seem to bother Kathryn. She sat transfixed as scene after scene flickered by, each beginning innocuously enough with a mistaken identity, the ordering of a pizza, a hopeful job interview, then progressed, with alarming rapidity Payne noted, into myriad breathtaking coital acrobatics.

Each successive coupling was accompanied by Kathryn's low, shuddering groans, and more than once she pressed pause on the VCR and pointed toward the frozen image, grinning a Cheshire grin. Payne, sitting beside her on sofa, grinned and groaned in response, but felt somehow let down by the whole thing. He noticed early on that not only the dialogue but also several of the visuals were running on a loop.

When Kathryn finally decided on a segment, rewound it and watched it twice, and said with her now customary throatiness, "Ooh, let's try that one, naughty boy," Payne felt a shiver of fear run down his spine.

He remained sitting on the sofa as she climbed down onto the throw rug in front of the television and slipped out of her panties and bra. He marvelled at the determination on her face as she closely studied the frozen image on the screen, twisting her limbs so that they matched the rather uncomfortable-looking contortions of the actress in the video—the same actress, Payne realized, who graced the cover of the cassette. Where are her wooden shoes, he wondered.

"Well?" Kathryn said, her head turned awkwardly back over her shoulder, looking as if she'd just gone through a severe chiropractic manipulation.

"Sorry?"

"It's your turn now," she said and grinned another grin, this one as crooked as her body. "I can't stay like this forever, you know."

Payne stood up from the sofa and, as he slowly lowered his boxers, was gripped by an overwhelming sensation that seemed to come at him from the darkest shadows of his past. He felt himself back in the boys' locker room of his old high school. *We all shower, Mr Payne,* came Coach Foster's voice through the mist. *Now off with your drawers.*

"For Christ's sake, Harvey," Kathryn said. "Hurry up. I think I'm getting a cramp."

Payne took a deep breath and swallowed hard, then stepped out of his underpants, almost certain that the laughter and wet towel ends would follow in the wake of his old gym teacher's echoing words. He even flinched when Kathryn reached out and touched his shin.

"Come on, let's go," she purred.

Keeping an eye on the television, Payne lowered himself onto one knee. The throw rug, he noticed immediately, was very rough against his flesh, almost as if he had just knelt on splintery wood. Already, in this the earliest stage of positioning, he appreciated the dexterity of the actor motionless before him. Then, stretching out his other leg to full length, in the same manner he remembered having seen a back catcher for the Baltimore Orioles do, Payne felt a tightening in the back of his knee, as if an elastic had been stretched to its limit. Still, he proceeded, and took hold of Kathryn's left ankle and brought it to rest on his shoulder.

"Almost there," she whispered, as she fitted her right leg into the empty triangle of space created by his outstretched thighs. "Now, get in closer."

Payne, a sheen of sweat forming on his brow, began to shuffle forward, finding it not only difficult to keep his balance, but also somewhat painful, as the carpet grazed the skin from his knee. In place finally, and not more than a little out of breath, he hunkered slightly, so as to bring his hips onto the same plane as Kathryn's. It was then he felt the sharp snap. It did not, however, occur in the strained ligaments behind his extended knee, as he had expected.

"What's wrong?" Kathryn asked, perturbed.

"Something . . ."

"Well, what?"

". . . in my back." Payne groaned, as frozen in place as the far more flexible actors on the television. "Something's happened . . . in my back."

"What already?"

"I don't know . . ."

Kathryn shifted.

"Ouch," Payne yelped. "Please don't . . . can't move."

Kathryn moaned and Payne could see out of the corner of his eye that she was wriggling the toes of her foot propped on his shoulder.

"Oh, Harvey," she whined. "You're going to have to. I can't feel my leg."

"Just give it a second," he begged. "Something's slipped, I think. I just need a second."

Payne tried to adjust himself to relieve the pressure on his bent knee but succeeded only in igniting a fire in his lower spine.

"Please, Harvey," Kathryn said, an edge in her voice. "I'm getting a pain in my hip now."

Suddenly there were other voices in the room, moaning and gasping and calling out. Payne, frightened, twisted around to see who'd walked in on them and as he did felt the cold blade of agony tear up his spine and prise apart his shoulder blades. As he fell sidelong onto the rough throw rug, which he now in a flash resolved to pitch into the garbage, Payne recalled the ancient Norse tradition of the "Bloody Eagle," which involved the cutting open of an enemy's back so as to expose the heart and lungs to the cold air. And as he cautiously reached around to feel the warm sponginess of his displaced organs, he heard Kathryn's laughter.

She was leaning against the sofa, massaging her tingling leg with one hand and pointing toward the television with the other. The pause button had cut out, and on the screen the two actors were performing with ease and obvious pleasure the act that now left Payne in paroxysms of Nordic anguish.

Payne, feeling the muscles in his lower back, just to the right of his spine, curling up into a hot little fist, arched his shoulders in the hope of unclenching them. He'd been expecting the discomfort at some point, what with having to sit for so long, especially in the confining seats of coach class. He'd already grown accustomed to the dull, slow-burning ache that had visited him with regularity since the fiasco with the video. If he was in his office working and it came upon him, he would lay himself down on the floor with his arms outstretched, crucifix-like, and wait out the spasm. He'd even done this once on the cold linoleum tiles of his kitchen floor when a particularly intense knurl formed as he was tending to a large pot of angel-hair pasta. But the prospect of lying supine in the aisle of economy class was unlikely. It was not simply his humility that prevented him; the remarkable narrowness of the aisle made such an act impossible.

It was the doctor in the emergency ward who suggested lying on the floor to him. The embarrassment of that visit reddened Payne's cheeks even now. The most difficult thing had been getting his clothes back on. He had to remain lying on his side while Kathryn pulled on his underpants, gently rolling him onto his back only when it came time to slide them over his hips. The doctor hadn't been nearly so gentle when he pulled them halfway down his buttocks so that he could get a good look at the affected area.

"And you say you did this moving an armoire?" Payne remembered the doctor saying, his voice flush with doubt. "Must have twisted yourself into an extraordinarily awkward position. And what about the abrasions on your knee and cheek?"

"Fell down," Payne replied. "When I twisted myself."

"Yes, I see," the doctor said, again with suspicion, casting a quick glance toward Kathryn. "Of course," he continued, patting Payne on the belly, "if you got rid of a bit of this you wouldn't have near so much trouble. The abdomen and the back should act as counterbalances, you see. It shouldn't be a case of one supporting the other."

Payne remembered the look on Kathryn's face as she stood there, her back brushing up against the plastic curtain of the examination carrel. The doctor explained that it wasn't anything serious, a pull of the latissimus and probably the ilio-costalis, as well—nothing that rest and heat wouldn't cure. As he said this, Payne saw slight traces of distaste reflected in Kathryn's eyes, as if she was being forced to watch something that, although organic, was also unsightly, like childbirth or death. What had been missing from her expression, though, Payne was now willing to admit, was compassion.

That was the beginning of it, Payne now realized, and thought about how it was that examining rooms figured so prominently in his declines.

He gazed up at the television monitor. The little white airplane had exceeded the apex of its arc, which passed just south of Greenland, and was dipping now toward the Irish coast.

———〰———

During the week that he was laid up, Kathryn came to him with heating pads and hot packs of various shapes, sizes and consistencies. Of the electric heating pads Payne was wary, afraid that if he happened to spill the orange juice he kept on his bedside table he might inadvertently electrocute himself. He was much more confident with the Presto-Relief Hot-Cold Compresses: small plastic pouches filled with a gelatinous blue slime that could be put in the freezer to cool or popped in the microwave to warm up. He liked the way they moulded themselves to his back and his neck, which had begun to stiffen with the extended bed rest.

Payne found that he enjoyed convalescing, looked forward each day to Kathryn's coming around to check on him. He took pleasure in watching the way she moved about the bedroom, picking up his knocked-over juice cups and clearing away plates of dried sandwich crusts and toast ends and plastic soda-biscuit wrappers. And to have her climb into bed beside him and rub minty-smelling analgesic on his back took him to new heights of arousal, so much so that when Kathryn tried to roll him over, he would feign agony and urge her to apply more ointment.

Payne was glad, too, to be shed of his lecturing and tutorial obligations for a few weeks, passing the latter off to an eager TA. He used his time to reacquaint himself with poor neglected Noel Gaynor, sifting through his collection of Xeroxed miscellany, rereading his doctoral thesis and the pared-down academic article he'd had such trouble getting published—all of which he coerced Kathryn into carting home from his office.

With a vigour he had not demonstrated since gaining tenure, Payne rededicated himself to his dream of transforming "Lost in the Bush" from treatment to book-length treatise. He threw himself into his work; at first he lay on the bed, with his notes spread out across the duvet, and then, after his back started to come around, he hunched over the kitchen table, scribbling in old-fashioned marble-covered writing tablets. He filled page after page with musings on Gaynor's life in England, extrapolating from fact. He pestered the chief librarian at the college into sending a courier with precious archival material. He began to annotate both volumes of fiction, convincing himself of the possibility that he could publish them as a collected edition along with the letters, with himself as editor, of course. From there it would be a short step to getting it and his companion book on Gaynor's life and work onto the course list at Severn, and from Severn like wildfire to institutions all across the country. It was as if, huddled in his kitchen with a warm Presto-Relief Hot-Cold Compress tucked under the waistband of his boxers, Payne could finally see the light of redemption glowing just off in the distance, just as Gaynor must have when he looked out toward the blackness of the Algonquin bush.

So immersed had Payne become that he took little notice of the change in Kathryn. On into his second week of recuperation she still came every day, but arrived later in the afternoon and left earlier in the evening. She did not share Payne's enthusiasm for his subject, and would sit quietly by while he conjectured about Gaynor's life with Penelope, about how stifling the monotony of their marriage must have been to drive him to seek contentment in a wild and untamed world. And when, in the middle of one of his flights, she rose from the sofa and took up her backpack and car keys, he broke off and asked where she was off to so early.

"It's Professor Foden. He's got us doing papers."

"Really?" Payne said, distracted. "What on?"

"Oh, you know," Kathryn smiled, rummaging through her bag. "The Greeks. Aristophanes."

When she called the next afternoon to say that she wouldn't be able to come by, Payne thought nothing of it. He was deep into Catharine Parr Traill's *The Female Emigrant's Guide*, marking passages he felt both infantile and arrogant and preparing a counter-argument with material taken directly from one of Gaynor's unsent letters. But the following evening, when he looked up from the table and saw that it was past eleven and he hadn't heard from her, he became worried.

The answering service picked up on her cellphone, but he didn't leave a message. Instead, he hung up and the dialled her apartment. He could feel an immense knot forming in his lower back as he listened to the faraway ringing, and he reached around and did his best to knead it away. Payne was just about to hang up when she answered.

"Hello?"

"Kathryn?"

"Yes."

"Are you all right? You sound out of breath."

"No, I'm fine."

"Then why are you panting?"

"I . . . I'm working out."

Payne could hear her trying to steady her breathing.

". . . I just finished doing some sit-ups . . . I'm a little winded."

"Oh?"

There was silence on the line.

"Is everything okay?" Payne asked.

"Yes. Why wouldn't it be?"

"Well, I thought that you'd be coming by. Or maybe call."

"Sorry about that, Harvey. I got caught up."

"With exercise?"

"What?"

"You got caught up with exercise?"

"Yes. No. I mean, the paper. I got caught up with the paper for . . . for Professor Foden."

"Oh, the Aristophanes?"

"Sorry?"

"The Aristophanes. The Greeks."

There was another long silence.

"Uh-huh," Kathryn said. "That's right. The Greeks."

———〰———

It now felt to Payne as if he was the only person left awake on the airplane. Even the flight attendants had disappeared into the curtained galley, no doubt to get some rest before it came time to hand out breakfast to the passengers.

He leaned his head back and questioned whether or not it all wasn't a mistake, if he wouldn't have been better off just sending his regrets to Professor Hefflin. Thanks, but no thanks. But then, what difference would it have made? The options open to him were decidedly limited: alone in a hotel room in Hoogeveen or alone in his house in Severn. Either way he was still alone.

Payne brushed his hand across the fabric of the empty seat beside him. There was something in it strangely reminiscent of the throw rug on the floor in front of his television set. And, he wondered, if he rubbed hard enough, could he scrape the skin from his palm?

—ᴍ—

He'd tried to get back to work after talking to Kathryn, but his concentration was broken. He began to imagine her in tight bicycle shorts, sleeveless shirt, bands on her wrists and head. And perspiring from exertion. It was true she could stand to lose a pound or two. But it wasn't a slimmer, trimmer version of Kathryn that worked on his thoughts; rather, it was the possibility of her slick, salty skin. Payne could almost taste it on his tongue. He packed up his work and found his jacket and boots.

Kathryn lived in downtown Severn, in one of the old rundown office buildings off the main street that had been converted by its owner into cramped flats suitable to student budgets. Kathryn's apartment was on the second floor, and her window overlooked an alleyway that the tenants used for parking.

When Payne drove in, there were only two cars there: Kathryn's battered Celica and a red Saab. He pulled in behind the Saab. On the way over he had decided that rather than buzz up, he would climb the fire escape and surprise her. He gave only a momentary thought to how this might frighten her, deciding instead that a chivalrous entrance through her bedroom window could lead to some intriguing role-playing once they'd disrobed.

It was bitterly cold outside and what little snow there was lay like plaster dust on the pavement, with a few stray flakes twisting through the night air. Payne had to climb atop an overturned garbage pail to reach the release for the fire-escape stairs. They emitted a rusty screech as he lowered them, and the metal was icy to the touch. He should have worn his gloves. He tried to be as quiet as possible as he climbed. Through the window on the first landing he saw the flickering of a television and he moved quickly to the next flight of metal steps. Near the top he stopped a moment to catch his breath and decided that maybe he should start thinking about exercise too.

On reaching the second landing he found Kathryn's window dark and wondered if she hadn't already gone to bed. He had second thoughts about his plan. The idea was rather careless and impulsive, completely out of character, which was why he had liked it. It was a way of showing Kathryn that he was open to risk, was willing to take a chance, things she had on occasion accused him of being unable to do. Now he wasn't so sure. What if someone had seen him skulking up the fire escape looking into windows? They would, no doubt, call the police—Kathryn might even call the police herself, and she'd have every right. It was ridiculous to be peeping into her window in the middle of the night. And what would people at the college think if he was caught creeping about? Payne realized that he could go on all night debating the foolishness of his position, that anyone who knew him would expect as much. So he took a deep breath and decided to carry on. But just as he was about to knock on the window, he caught sight of movement from inside. His eyes were beginning to adjust to the darkness and he pressed his face against the glass. In the bed in the far corner of the room he saw the blankets shift. She must be having trouble getting to sleep, Payne thought, and decided that it was unfair of Gil Foden to put his students through the stress of a term paper so close to the holidays. And then the covers were thrown back and there was Foden himself, one hand clamped on Kathryn's left breast, the other gripping the headboard of the bed, his bare white arse bouncing up and down in the gloom.

Payne shuddered, felt immediately sick to his stomach, but was unable to move away from the window. His back began to tighten. He could hear their voices, or at least imagined that he could. There was Kathryn's: the purr, the moan, the throatiness he'd assumed she saved only for him. Now he heard it calling out Foden's name, urging him, encouraging, giving directions. And then, ridiculously, Payne realized that she hadn't been exercising at all, and just as the thought crossed his mind, he laughed at the obviousness of it. And for a moment he felt sorry that he'd not had the chance to see her in tight bicycle shorts.

He remained kneeling on the landing until they'd finished, somewhat surprised that Foden's climax was not the victorious outcry he'd expected, but a rather pathetic collapse into exhaustion. Then Payne turned and started back down the fire escape, no longer concerned now about the noise he made.

On the way to his car he stopped beside the Saab, noticing now the faculty parking pass stuck to the inside of its windshield.

For almost an hour he sat in his car, his head back against the rest, looking out at the night sky. His mind was awash with images, yet at the same time he could bring none into clear focus. He had never been beaten up before, but he was fairly certain this was what it felt like: his body ached all over. And his stomach felt empty, as if he hadn't eaten in days.

He rolled his head to the side and noticed on the passenger seat the thick volume of Victoriana he had meant to drop off at the college library that afternoon. The librarian had called his house twice during the week requesting its return. Payne picked it up and got out of the car.

The book was oversized and weighed close to ten pounds. It had stiff leather boards and gilt edging. It was more a curio than a scholarly work. It had been published privately in London in the 1880s and was distributed to institutions and moneyed collectors. This edition had been bequeathed to Severn College by one of its benefactors and was kept in the reserve stacks in the basement of the library. The librarian had been very adamant that it be handled with care.

Even with the book being so heavy, Payne thought he might need a running start. So he took a few steps back before he lifted it over his head. It shattered the driver's side window of the Saab with ease and bounced off the steering wheel before coming to rest, tent-like, over the gearshift. The car alarm sounded immediately: horn blaring, lights flashing.

Payne walked calmly to his car and backed out of the alleyway as lights began appearing in the apartment windows above.

—⟿—

Sleepers, including Payne's neighbour, were beginning to awaken. Shades were raised, arms stretched and toiletries gathered to freshen up before the plane's arrival in Amsterdam. As for Payne, he hadn't slept a wink. He'd spent the last hour thinking about the grovelling message he'd left on the answering service of Kathryn's cellphone—she'd had the number for her apartment changed after he'd called for a week straight, each time hanging up after two rings.

Among other things, more clichés than he cared to recall, he'd said that he forgave her. And he was certain that had he not been in the crowded departure terminal, he would have actually cried. He was thankful he hadn't. He could just imagine the two of them, Gil Foden and Kathryn, lying naked on her bed with their heads pressed together listening to him weeping and snuffling back his snotty heartbreak. He was glad now that at least he hadn't given them that added satisfaction.

Out of the corner of his eye he saw the little man in grey shift in his seat. Payne unfastened his seat belt and when he felt the soft touch of a hand on his elbow he roughly brushed it away.

"Please," he muttered, and stepped into the aisle. "I insist."

The man looked at him, almost frightened, and Payne felt a gratifying flush of power. He even leaned into the man as he struggled to squeeze by. Then Payne settled back down in his seat and looked up at the television monitor. There were still forty-two minutes until arrival at Amsterdam.

And then what? Payne wondered. He looked at the closed notebook in his lap, then passed his hand again across the stiff fabric of the empty seat beside him.

Simple, he thought, and then nothing.

AN IRISH HOLIDAY

THE COTTAGE STOOD AT THE END of a winding gravel drive that was bordered by rhododendron and meandered its way up a gentle slope from the roadway below. A ragged grove of silver birch stretching out along the foot of the property hid passing cars from view, but it did little to dampen their noise, which came like an angry drone through the thin-leafed trees.

"Sure it's peaceful come evening," the landlord said, as he fitted the key into the lock of the cottage's front door. "No traffic to speak of, really."

They smiled politely, but said nothing, waiting to be shown inside. The landlord's name was Mr Monaghan, with a hard g, he'd told them, and although he'd waited for them for more than an hour, he did not seem put off by their late arrival from the airport. On the contrary, he was overly cordial when the taxi finally dropped them at the roadside below. He'd helped to collect their luggage from the trunk of the car and made friendly inquiries as to the comfort of their journey, doing his utmost, it seemed to David, to endear himself.

Mr Monaghan paused a moment on the threshold and fished a palmful of coins from his trouser pocket. Selecting one, he inserted it into the slot in a large metal box affixed to the wall just inside the door, then twisted a dial set below, illuminating the entranceway. Turning, he noticed the expressions on their faces.

"I'm sure they mentioned that the lights work off a timer." He smiled.

David looked at Rebecca, then shook his head.

"Did they not now?" Mr Monaghan said. "My apologies, then. You see, electricity is rather dear. Now the refrigerator, of course, runs constantly. But I'm afraid for the lights you'll need to feed the register. It really is far more economical this way."

"Yes," Rebecca said. "I'm sure that it is."

Mr Monaghan smiled again: "Now, if you'll just come through," he said, a welcoming arm outstretched, "I'll show you about. Ahead there," he indicated with a nod and a discreet tone, "we have the toilet. The *bathroom*, I believe you call it."

After showing them the rest of the cottage, which consisted of a small lounge with incongruous rattan furniture, a cramped kitchenette fronted by a bamboo lattice and two small bedrooms opposite the toilet, Mr Monaghan made to leave.

"Ah, yes. I should mention," he said, standing in the front doorway, "there's an immersion heater in the closet. You'll be needing to turn that on if you've thoughts of having a shower. Now, if you find yourself wanting anything else," he continued, smiling still, "I've left my card on the kitchen counter. Feel free to call me any time after 6 p.m.".

For a moment after he left, David and Rebecca remained standing in the entranceway, staring at the empty door frame. Then Rebecca went to the closet and investigated the water heater.

"It takes coins, as well," she said.

"I'm not surprised," replied David.

"Do you have any Irish money?"

"Only bills."

"You shouldn't have tipped the taxi driver."

David bent down and picked up their suitcases. "It's a little late for that now," he said, then looked between the two bedrooms. "Which do you think? Front or back?"

"It'll be quieter in the back," she said.

Rebecca remained in the entranceway, vainly searching her pocketbook for the proper coins, while David took the luggage into the bedroom. He returned shaking his head, and walked past her to glance into the other bedroom.

"What's the matter?"

"I didn't even notice."

"Notice what?"

"That man talked so much, I didn't even see it."

"What didn't you see?"

"The beds," David said. "They're singles."

"You're joking."

"Look for yourself."

"I don't want to look," she said, closing her purse. "What are we supposed to do? There's no way we'll both fit into a single bed."

"Don't worry about it." David began to roll up his sleeves. "I'll just take apart the one in the front bedroom and move it into the back."

"Oh, leave it be, for now," Rebecca sighed. "Why don't you go down the road and see if there's anywhere you can get change."

"You want to take a shower?"

"Yes, that. And I'm sure we'll need the lights, too."

———⚲———

David and Rebecca Marsden had agreed to take the cottage for the entire month of August. A good long vacation. Enough time away to get things sorted out. Rebecca hadn't had to worry about work since leaving her job at the bank. And David, who taught English at a private school, was on summer break anyhow. So it was never a question of opportunity.

At first, when they began to discuss the possibility of the trip, they'd considered previous destinations. Paris, where they'd spent their honeymoon thirteen years earlier, initially came to David's mind. But Rebecca balked at the idea, on account of it being far too expensive. He suspected, though, that her considerations were more than merely financial. In Paris they would be reminded of certain hopes they had once shared, and shared no longer. So too would be the case with Key West and Cancun and Venice and Madrid. And remaining in Canada, going either west to the Rockies or east to the Maritimes, was never contemplated. What they needed was a sense of foreignness.

It was David who proposed Ireland: for its greenery, he'd said. It was Rebecca who found the ad for the cottage in the classifieds at the back of a glossy magazine: *Quaint, secluded hillside cottage with all the modern amenities. Located in the picturesque seaside town of Bray, Co. Wicklow. Just thirty minutes from Dublin City Centre. Weekly/monthly rentals available.* The arrangements were made over the phone with an agency right in downtown Toronto, and all the particulars were posted to their home two weeks before they were due to leave. To economize, they'd booked themselves on a charter flight that had a two-hour layover at Shannon before heading on to Dublin.

Sitting on the tarmac at Shannon, David noticed Rebecca picking at her fingers. She'd forced the cuticles away from the nails and he could see a small gap between her flesh and the red acrylic polish. She had also torn thin strips from the sides of her fingertips, one leaving an angry weal that stretched down to the first knuckle. He could have stopped her by simply covering her hands with his own. But he knew that she would only start again when he took them away, so he didn't see the point. Instead, he turned and looked out the window and watched as the baggage handlers offloaded cargo containers from the belly of the plane.

—⚭—

It wasn't much of a cottage, David decided after he'd unpacked his suitcase, putting his clothes in the bottom two drawers of the lopsided bureau, leaving the top two for Rebecca. Rather, it was a fairly cheaply constructed bungalow: lath and plaster, covered by a thin coat of yellow stucco. When Rebecca had read the advertisement to him, he'd pictured solid stone walls, thick lintels over doors and windows, a thatched roof, a wide hearth and blackened fireplace. There was a hearth, but it was narrow, and the fire was a three-bar heater that resembled an electric toaster cut down the middle.

He stayed up late the first night, sitting in the lounge reading the novel he'd begun on the plane. He found it difficult to concentrate; he was rarely able to complete a book begun in transit, but also he had no idea how long the timer on the lights would last. Rebecca had gone to bed as soon as they'd returned from dinner.

They had followed the road back toward town, a walk that took them past quiet terraced houses and along the bank of a deep, slow-moving river. There they stopped a moment. On a narrow island in the middle stood a derelict building. It was three storeys high and ran the length of the island, which looked to David to be as long as a city block. Its grey stones were crumbling and moss covered, and its roof was caved in, leaving only a hollow shell of walls and empty windows.

"What do you suppose it was?" Rebecca asked.

"A workhouse, maybe."

She looked at him as he spoke, then turned quickly away.

"You mean," she said, and David caught the slight trace of fear in her voice, "like the kind they used to send children to?"

"No," he quickly countered. "No, that's not what I meant. I'm just saying it was probably some sort of factory, that's all."

Rebecca continued to stare at the ruins.

"If you like," David offered, laying an awkward hand on her shoulder, "I'll ask someone when we get to town."

"No," she said, and started walking again.

They ate in the restaurant of the Royal Hotel, at a table near the window so they could look out onto the high street. Leek soup to start, followed by Atlantic salmon baked in airy pastry and a Sauvignon Blanc suggested by the wine steward. But Rebecca, who'd complained of her hunger on the taxi ride from the airport, ate little. David watched as she used her fork to dissect the pastry layer by layer, flake by flake, until she was left with only the pink meat. This too she anatomized, separating it along the sinew. David said nothing, finishing his own meal. Afterward he declined the waiter's offerings from the dessert trolley and ordered a coffee for himself.

Outside, Rebecca complained of a headache and sent him back into the hotel lobby to order a taxi so they wouldn't have to walk. On the drive back to the cottage, she leaned her head against the window and closed her eyes. She kept them closed until she was certain they'd passed the ruined factory, though it had grown so dark that David could not make it out in the night.

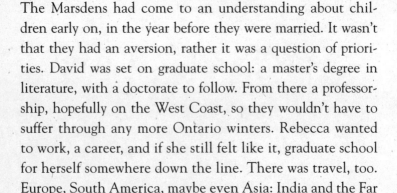

The Marsdens had come to an understanding about children early on, in the year before they were married. It wasn't that they had an aversion, rather it was a question of priorities. David was set on graduate school: a master's degree in literature, with a doctorate to follow. From there a professorship, hopefully on the West Coast, so they wouldn't have to suffer through any more Ontario winters. Rebecca wanted to work, a career, and if she still felt like it, graduate school for herself somewhere down the line. There was travel, too. Europe, South America, maybe even Asia: India and the Far East. None of which could be done with children in tow.

For a while, they had a dog. A mutt named Buster. He filled the hole, as David put it. Many a Saturday in the summer, they would spend the day with him in High Park. He was a big friendly hound. Children would come up to him and scratch behind his ears while he licked the ice-cream cones and ate the hot dogs they held in their hands; and if their hands were empty, he would make do with their faces, passing his big lazy tongue over their noses and mouths. When they travelled, Buster was boarded at a veterinary clinic on Bloor Street, and was as happy to go as he was to return. They'd had him just over two years on the cold November night that he ran out the front door and was killed by the neighbour's car. Although he never said as much to Rebecca, David greeted the dog's death with a measure of release.

David Marsden slept on the narrow rattan sofa the first night. The second he spent in the front bedroom, in the single bed that he'd yet to move, waking late on their third morning in Ireland to the smell of burnt toast. He found Rebecca sitting in one of the matching rattan armchairs with the floral-patterned cushions. Her knees were pulled up to her chest. She was crying.

"What's the matter?"

"Oh, it's that goddamn toaster," she said, wiping away tears with the back of her hand. "That's the third time it's burned."

"Maybe you should watch it, then," David said. He walked across to the kitchenette and removed the two blackened pieces of bread from the toaster and dropped them into the bin with the other four. Then he looked at his wife through the bamboo lattice and smiled: "At least we don't have to pay by the slice."

Rebecca did not return his smile. She stared straight ahead and began to rock back and forth. David came out from the kitchenette and knelt in front of the chair. He gently took hold of her ankles.

"Listen, honey," he said, trying to soften his hoarse morning voice. "It's only toast. There's no need to get upset. We'll just go out for breakfast."

"It's not the bloody toast, David."

"Well, then what is it?" he said, letting go of her ankles.

Rebecca looked him in the face and David had to fight the urge to wipe away the thin trickle of snot that leaked from her nose.

"What are we doing here?" she asked, her voice as timid as a child's. "That's what it is: I want to know what we are doing here."

David stood up and started toward the door. Halfway there he stopped and turned back round.

"We're on holiday," he said. "That's what we're doing here."

—⁂—

Getting his master's degree had proved more difficult than David Marsden had expected. His Ph.D. proved too much. Unable to complete his dissertation, he withdrew from the program and began to look for work, a search that finally ended at Thornecliffe College, an exclusive school west of the city. And while it wasn't true academia, it at least had the patina of academia: old, red-brick buildings with ivy-covered walls and a wide, green, well-manicured quadrangle where the students lounged about or played pickup games of soccer and rugby. If he glanced up quickly while he was crossing from the administration building to the upper-school block, he could imagine he was strolling the Hart House Green toward Philosopher's Walk. But the facade was soon broken when he entered his classroom and looked into the blank faces of the fifteen- and sixteen-year-old boys in his charge. Not even their expensive navy blazers could hide the fact that they were no more than bored teenagers.

The money wasn't much either, so Rebecca had to put thoughts of her own education on hold and stay on at the bank. She did well, being promoted regularly. She rose from teller to assistant loan officer and finally to mortgage manager. Before she left, there was talk of her getting her own branch.

Although their plans had gone somewhat astray, they found themselves comfortable. And for a time, even content.

—∞—

The previous day they'd taken the train into Dublin and sought out the places they might like to explore more fully in the coming weeks. They walked through St Stephen's Green and across the great cobbled quadrangle of Trinity College. They noted the visiting hours at the university library when the public was admitted to see the *Book of Kells*. They stood on the O'Connell Street Bridge and gazed into the Liffey, David hoping to catch a glimpse of a pamphlet floating on the murky waters. For dinner they went to Davy Byrne's and were disappointed to find the pub crowded with American tourists. But on the whole, it had been a very good day. Rebecca laughed a great deal, and it pleased David to see her happy.

Her mood didn't last. It darkened with the evening and carried through into the next day, so that as they set about to investigate Bray itself, the outing felt more like an obligation than an adventure.

They reached the seafront by taking a side street down from the Royal Hotel and found a breakwall esplanade that stretched the length of a vast beach. The tide was out so far that the distant water looked more like a mirage than the Irish Sea. The noonday sun was strong, and David regretted not having worn his shorts; his jeans felt heavy in the heat. Rebecca wore a pale yellow cotton sundress, sleeveless and loose fitting. The soft wind off the water rippled its hem, gently lifting it above her knees. David watched her as she walked on ahead of him. Her hair, dark with a hint of auburn, had started to come loose from the ponytail she'd tied it in, and strands of it were being picked up by the breeze and fluttered about in the air above her head. The sun had begun to bring the freckles on her shoulders to the surface. As she moved she swung her arms lazily at her side, more like a young girl than a grown woman. From her wrist her instant camera dangled on its tether, bumping clumsily against her thigh with each step. She stopped walking when she noticed he was no longer at her side, and turned to look at him.

"What's the matter with you?" she said, a hand held over her eyes to shield them from the sun.

"It's you," David said.

"What about me?"

"You look so beautiful." He stepped forward and reached out his hand. "Give me the camera. I want to take your picture."

But her face hardened and she held the camera tightly against her stomach.

"No," she said coldly. "I don't want my picture taken."

David led them down the wrong path. They had decided that before visiting the arcades along the esplanade, they would climb to the cross at the top of Bray Head. The guidebook David carried with him said that the panoramic view offered by the promontory was surpassed only by that of Glendalough farther inland in the Wicklow Mountains. He'd been eager to make the ascent, and in his eagerness had followed the trail that ran along the coast, rather than the one that curled around back of the bluff.

After half an hour of walking, with the cross far behind them and the trail ahead winding away into the distance, Rebecca refused to go on. She stood in the middle of the gravel track, her arms slack at her side.

"This isn't the way, David."

He glanced back at her, then turned and looked at where the trail, like a grey snake slithering along the cliffside, passed over a railway tunnel and disappeared behind the next hill.

"I don't know," he said. "Maybe it doubles back on itself around that bend."

Rebecca laughed sourly. "I don't care if it does," she said, shaking her head. "I'm not walking any farther."

"Look, I'm sure it won't take much longer. Why don't we just follow it around the bend and see? If it doesn't go anywhere, then we'll head back."

Rebecca folded her arms across her chest, then turned toward the slope.

"If you really want to get to the top of the hill so bad," she said, "then why don't we just climb the bloody thing?"

David followed her gaze.

"Looks pretty steep."

"Oh, for God's sake, David. I'll climb it by myself, then."

He watched her as she lifted the hem of her sundress and stepped over the low stone wall that separated the trail from the slope. She took great, long strides as she climbed, bringing her knees up close to her chest, then slamming her feet down forcefully. He was reminded again of a small girl, this time one that, having been scolded and sent to her room, shows her displeasure by thumping up the stairs. There was also a picturesque beauty in her ascent: her yellow dress fluttering among the shifting green grasses of the hill gave the impression of a lone bloom in a flowerless meadow. David again regretted not having the camera. But then Rebecca lost her footing; she wobbled to one side and held her arms out for balance. For the briefest moment it appeared that she'd regained her poise. Then she fell. David remained standing on the trail until he heard her sobs.

He hadn't climbed ten feet before he realized that the hill was far steeper than even he had thought, and when he grabbed at the ground to try and pull himself up, it felt as if he'd thrust his hands into a fire. The entire hillside, he now saw, as he blew on his palms, was blanketed in nettles. When he finally reached Rebecca she was on her feet again, holding her arms straight out in front of her. Already, angry red welts had begun to blossom on the soft white flesh of her forearms. Another stretched down her neck, from just below her ear to her collarbone.

"Goddamn you, David," she said, tears dripping from her chin.

"Sweetheart," David said, reaching out to wipe them away. "I'm so sorry. Really, I am."

"No, David. Goddamn you."

—⟨⟩—

The call from the hospital came while he was going over preps for the final examination with his twelfth-grade literature class. It was early June and outside the warm rays bathing the quadrangle seemed at odds with the tempestuousness of Lear's heath. They were reluctant to offer information, just said that Rebecca had been admitted to St Joseph's Medical Centre and that she was asking for him. The bank was in his mind the whole time as he raced back to the city: a robbery, violence.

When Rebecca told him, David had not known what to say. He'd held her hand tightly in his own, had kissed it, had kissed her forehead, had brushed away the strands of her hair that stuck to her damp brow. He'd stroked her arm, softly touching the inside of her elbow around the surgical tape that held the intravenous needle in place. He'd cried when she cried and cradled her head against his chest. The whole time wondering if his words of comfort sounded as hollow to Rebecca as they did to himself, if she could hear in them the sense of relief that he tried so to disguise.

—⟨⟩—

Rebecca left David sitting on the terrace of one of the many restaurants that crowded the esplanade and went back to the cottage alone.

When they'd arrived, the waitress had brought Rebecca a glass of ice and advised her to rub the cubes over her welts.

"It'll take the sting out, that will," she said. "But the red won't go till morning, so long as you don't scratch at 'em."

She'd done as instructed and the pain began to subside, only to be replaced by a terrible itch. David didn't bother with the ice. While they waited for their drinks, he studied the welts that had come up on his own skin, on the heels of his palms and across his wrists. Looking more closely, he could see tiny white thorns embedded in his flesh. When he held his hands up for Rebecca to see, she turned away from him.

The terrace was crowded with umbrellaed tables, most of them occupied by people having an early dinner after a long day spent on the beach or walking the trails around Bray Head. The din of the surrounding conversations seemed all the more conspicuous by the absence of any at the Marsdens' table. Rebecca ignored her plate of scampi and chips in favour of the dwindling glass of ice cubes, while David worked away unenthusiastically at his shepherd's pie. As soon as he could catch the waitress's eye, he ordered another pint of Guinness.

The day had begun to cool with the approach of evening and David could feel the familiar prickle of sunburn on his forehead. The thought of getting burnt had never even occurred to him, but looking around at those that had come from the beach, their skin bronzed or painfully pink, it seemed obvious.

As the waitress returned to take their plates away, a young German family sat down at the table to their left: a husband and wife, near to Rebecca and David's age, and two small children, a boy and a girl. The mother made a point of separating her children, seating them on opposite sides of the table. Then she spoke directly to each, issuing instructions so softly that even the hard edge of her accent was smoothed. The children nodded in turn and sat completely still while their mother filled two bottles from a Thermos of fruit juice she'd withdrawn from her knapsack. Her children content, the woman turned to her husband and, with her head held close to his, began to study the menu.

As David looked on, the little girl, whose chair faced away from him, leaned to the side, so that her head and shoulders were in view. She had fine blond curly hair and chubby arms. Her lashes were almost as pale as her eyes, and her cheeks ruddy from the sun. It took David a moment to realize that she was staring at him, and when he did, he became nervous, uncertain how to respond. Then the little girl slowly lifted her hand and, scrunching up her fat little fingers, offered him a wave. David, doing his best to smile, waved back.

When he turned away he saw that Rebecca had been watching him, the emptiness in her expression so complete it was as if she were no longer there.

Then she slowly stood up from the table.

"I'm going back," she said quietly, picking up the glass of ice. "You do what you want."

—◆◆◆—

David remained on the terrace as dusk gave way to evening, and with the coming darkness, the restaurant began to transform itself into a nightclub. The families and afternoon couples were replaced by groups of young men in jeans and khakis with loose polo shirts and short, shiny hair who huddled together with pint glasses in hand, staring after clutches of young women in tight slacks, short skirts and blouses unbuttoned at the neck. From inside the restaurant came the thump of dance music, its thick bass resonating in David's chest. He had looked out across the boulevard and the esplanade and watched the tide creep in with the waning of the sun. Since the harbour lay to the east, there was no splendid setting, just the impression of a blind being drawn.

As more young people arrived, David gave up his table and moved to a place near the entrance of the restaurant, a small corner between a wall and a planter where he could watch the goings-on. He looked on with feelings of both nostalgia and envy as those around him, loosened with drink, began to mingle more freely. Then, thinking of Rebecca back at the cottage alone, he decided to have one more pint before heading out.

Inside the restaurant, the bar was crowded and he had to force his way to the rail. With his drink finally in hand, he went outside again. There were fewer people on the terrace when he returned, the bulk having already made their way indoors to the dance floor that had been set up at the back of the restaurant.

Still holding his drink, David wandered down to the bottom of the terrace, to where two large bouncers guarded the narrow gateway that opened on to the sidewalk. As he approached, one politely held up his hand.

"Sorry, sir," he said, motioning to the beer in David's hand. "Can't take that with you."

David looked at his full glass. He took a drink and then set it on a table.

"Just having a last sip," he said. "I'm finished with it."

"That's good, then," the man said and crossed his heavy arms.

"I wonder if you can tell me something?" David said, feeling a little unsteady now.

The second bouncer narrowed his eyes at David.

"What would that be, then?" the first said, his attention divided.

"There's a building," David began. "On the other side of town. In the middle of a river. It's fallen down. Abandoned. Do you know the one?"

"Afraid not, sir."

"Oh," David said, nodding. "Just thought I'd ask."

The second bouncer looked at him again and stuck out his chin.

"What you want to know for?" he said.

"Just curious, really. I was wondering what it used to be?"

"That's the old paint factory," the man said, his tone harsh. "Goddamn awful place it was. When they was making red, the whole goddamn river went red. Like blood, it was."

"So it wasn't a workhouse, then?"

"A what?"

"Nothing," David said. "Never mind. Have a good night."

David could see the lights from the bottom of the drive. The cottage was lit up like a beacon on a hilltop. He made his way slowly, dragging his feet in the gravel so they made rasping sounds in the quiet night. The front door was unlocked and he shielded his eyes against the glare in the entranceway. With his free hand he felt for the wall switch and turned out the light, then he went to the back bedroom. It was empty. He found Rebecca curled up on the rattan sofa in the lounge. Her back was to him.

"Why have you got all the lights on?" he asked.

When she spoke her voice was thick and nasal, as if she had a cold.

"I wanted to make sure you could find your way home."

David could tell she had been crying. And when she rolled over he saw her nose was raw from blowing and her eyes puffy and red. He remained standing in the doorway for a moment longer, then went over and sat on the edge of the sofa. He ran his hand over her hair.

"I'm so sorry," he said. "Really. I wanted this to be different."

"You've been drinking," she said.

"Yes, a little."

She turned away from him again and wrapped her arms over her stomach. David took his hand from her hair. He glanced around the lounge and thought what an ugly place it was that they'd come to: the tacky furnishings, the cheap bamboo lattice hiding the kitchenette, the coin-operated lighting. It was perfunctory, seedy, like a roadside motel in a degenerate part of town. He wished they were somewhere else.

"I asked about the old building on the island," he said, because he could think of nothing else. "It used to be a paint factory."

"I don't care, David."

"No," he replied. "Nor me."

She reached out then and took his hand and placed it against her belly.

"I can't stop thinking about it," she said quietly.

"I know."

"Everything I see reminds me."

"Yes."

"When you looked at that little girl today I thought I would be sick. I wanted to scream. I wanted to hit that woman and take her child and run away."

David nodded his head and did not resist as she pushed his hand hard against her stomach, digging her nails into his flesh.

"And then, in my mind, I was back there again. Standing there in the middle of the bank with it running down my leg. Into my shoes. On the floor. Everyone staring at me. Pointing. Putting their hands over their mouths while it all ran away like goddamn piss down my legs."

"Don't, Rebecca," he said, feeling far away from her. "Don't do this to yourself."

She pushed his hand away and sat up, her eyes dry and angry now. She shook her head and laughed.

"To myself, David?" she said. "Is that what you think I'm doing?"

Rebecca got up from the sofa and crossed the little room and stood on the hearth. She looked down at the electric fire, its bars black and cold.

David went to her, put his arms around her from behind and rested his chin on her shoulder.

"It'll be fine," he said, close to her ear, her hair moving under his breath. "Everything will be okay again. We'll be okay again."

"No, David." She stiffened under his touch. "No, David," she said again. "No, I don't think we will."

IOSIF IN LOVE

ALEXANDER SVANIDZE LOOKED ACROSS the table at Iosif Vissarionovich Dzhugashvili. Even now, with three glasses of vodka drunk and the fourth ready to be tasted, he could not imagine this man a priest. It wasn't so much his friend's scruffy appearance: the patchy unkempt beard that struggled to hide his pallid complexion, the startling shock of raven hair, the rough threadbare coat or thin checkered scarf. It wasn't even the fierce black eyes that caught the faint flame of the gaslight burning on the wall opposite; the devil Rasputin himself has ferocious eyes, Alexander thought, and still he is a cleric, of sorts. This man, Iosif Vissarionovich, had been one short step removed from the ecclesiastic life: five years at the Tiflis seminary and just a single examination away from ordination. And yet Alexander simply could not envision him in the intricately embroidered cassock and absurd conical headdress of the church.

"Tell me, Koba," Alexander asked Iosif, "what was it like? The religious life?"

"Alyosha." The faint smile that had moments before curled
Iosif's lips disappeared and his mouth became no more than a
pencil line etched below his moustache. His voice had gone
cold, like a lump of coal pulled from the earth, thought
Alexander, feeling its chill.

"Alyosha," Iosif said again, his tone lighter this time,
and his smile returning. "I have told you, Alyosha, that I
do not wish to speak of the church. It is a hideout of
deceivers and hypocrites, backward-thinking old men who
pollute the minds of the workers with their hypothetical
God. All of them hand in pocket with the Tsar and his
sycophantic ministers, intent on keeping the proletariat
pinioned to the stinking earth with their pig-fattened
thumbs." As he spoke, Iosif's eyes grew darker still, even as
his smile widened, stretching the whiskers on his chin and
accentuating the randomness of his beard. "But do not
worry, Alyosha, my friend. In time they will be called to
answer for their liars' deeds. Then we shall see about this
saviour of theirs."

Iosif began to laugh as if he'd just divined the humour of
an elaborate joke, and Alexander watched in strange wonder
at the paradox that was his friend's face. In repose it had a
sternness that was frightening; it was not so much that it was
cruel, as simply, and disconcertingly, devoid of emotion. But
when Iosif laughed, his entire face crinkled; even his thick-
bridged Georgian nose scrunched up, giving him an almost
pixieish quality.

"You know, Koba," Alexander said, laying a hand across
Iosif's forearm, "it would not do to have Kato hear you talk
such."

Alexander knew that the mention of his sister would quiet Iosif, and quiet now was how he wanted him. Though revolutionary talk was rife in Tiflis, it was best kept behind closed doors—especially now that the *gendarmerie* had circulated their photographs. While he wouldn't admit it to Iosif, even being in this tavern unnerved him. That this quarter was sympathetic to the cause did not seem to help the matter. There were many ears about, not all of which, Alexander was certain, were so friendly that he and Iosif were safe from being turned over to the authorities for a fistful of kopecks.

Iosif, despite his best efforts, now wore the face of a fool, and looking at his friend, Alexander could tell that he was angry. Yet the buffoon that took up residence in Iosif's cheeks, adding to them traces of scarlet that not even the frigid winds of Irkutsk had been able to muster, would not allow this spleen to gain purchase.

"How is Yekaterina?" Iosif asked, an idiot-like shyness descending upon him.

Alexander lifted his glass to his mouth and as the vodka slid warmly over his tongue, offered a mockingly noncommittal shrug.

"Has she," Iosif said quietly, leaning forward, "asked about me?"

"My dear Koba," Alexander said, finding it was now his turn to smile, "you know how little our sweet Kato asks for."

Iosif could see he was being toyed with but refused to rise to the bait. "But me?" he whispered. "Has she anything to say about me?"

"Why don't you ask her yourself?" Alexander replied, pushing his empty glass into the middle of the table. "Come eat with us this evening."

For the briefest of moments, so fleeting that he thought he may have imagined it, Alexander saw worry flicker through his friend's black eyes. But Iosif was quick to recover himself, and with a cough he chased the anxiety away.

"I do not believe your mother would welcome my company," he said coolly. "She does not think highly of me, I am afraid."

"Koba," Alexander said as delicately as he could. "You, of all people, should know how little it matters what a mother thinks, if you will forgive my saying."

"True," Iosif replied. "Though I did not wish to say as much."

"I would have thought by now," Alexander said, laying his hand again on the other man's arm, "you would have realized that to me you can say anything. Besides," he continued, lowering his voice, "you must come. We need to talk about Erevan Square. If we're not careful, that Kamo will blow a hole in the middle of Tiflis. But this," he said, looking warily about, "is not the place to talk."

Iosif nodded. "You are right, of course," he replied, casting a glance at the men sitting at the surrounding tables. "No one is to be trusted."

———— ⟋⟋⟍ ————

"He is a pig," Alexander Svanidze's mother said to him as she lifted the heavy kettle from the iron stove-top. "Do you see him? The way he eats? Sucking the walnuts from his salad and leaving them on the side of his plate. Does he know the trouble it was to get those walnuts? Is he a squirrel collecting them for winter?"

Alexander looked back down the darkened corridor toward the sitting room; he could hear Iosif's annoyed voice. Things were not going well. He had not expected to see David Suliashvili sitting before the hearth with Yekaterina's hand in his own when he arrived home from the tavern. He was only thankful that Iosif had had errands to run and did not accompany him.

"Please, Mama," Alexander said in a hushed tone. "Please keep your voice down."

"Why?" she mocked. "Is the terrible Koba liable to silence me in my own home?"

Alexander glanced nervously at his mother. She had not seen Iosif Vissarionovich's temper, had not witnessed its swift and astonishing brutality. He left her then and made his way back along the murky passageway to the sitting room. There he found David Suliashvili sitting before the hearth again, but Yekaterina no longer sat beside him. His sister had moved to the rocking chair, where she sat with her embroidery, stitching the elaborate design into a traditional shawl that she hoped to sell at the Tiflis market. Alexander noticed, however, that the needlework did not command the whole of his sister's attention. Each time she drew the thread through the material she cast a glance across the room to where Iosif stood, one hand resting on the mantelshelf, the other gesticulating, using his newly affected ebony pipe to drive home the point he had just made about the Tsarists' betrayal of the people. Looking at his friend, Alexander could not help but feel the twinge of sympathy. Iosif, after their meeting in the tavern, had returned to the safe house to change his clothes in preparation to see Yekaterina, and he stood before them now wearing shiny black trousers and an oversized peasant blouse that, for all its bagginess, only served to accentuate the withering deformity that knurled his left arm. He had also trimmed his beard, but had done such a poor job of it, in nervous haste, Alexander imagined, that it appeared even more erratic. On his head he wore a Turkish fez, which, whether out of forgetfulness or intent, he had not removed during the whole of dinner. It seemed to be causing him some discomfort, but he made no move to relieve himself of it. In all, he cut a rather foolish figure; he looked a poseur. Yet Alexander could see that to Yekaterina he appeared anything but; when she looked at him, she did so with eyes filled with warmth and reverence; it was as if she was seeing not a shabbily dressed and awkward suitor, but a dashing brigand.

David saw this in Yekaterina's face as well and his own features in response became gloomy. Whereas a sulk on the face of some can make them strangely more attractive, it had the opposite effect on David. His petulance caused his bottom lip to fatten and his cheeks to sink into his skull; his eyes became hollow and his brow furrowed so that he looked a man much older than his twenty-five years: any semblance of his handsome dark-eyed, strong-jawed Georgian aspect vanished. He had turned himself out well in a sombre grey serge suit with a waistcoat and a white, buttoned shirt and black tie— the costume of the movement's intelligentsia, fashioned carefully after the clothes worn by Comrades Lenin and Trotsky. But he might as well have been wearing a burlap sack for all

Yekaterina noticed. He crossed his arms over his chest and stared at the floor.

From where he was standing in the doorway, Alexander could see that David was preparing to speak, and from the way he held his body, Alexander knew that what the other man had to say would be an incitement to Iosif. The two men had attended seminary together, and although they both eschewed the priesthood for the same cause, they had taken divergent paths: David now followed the path of thought, Iosif that of force. It had often put them at odds with one another. And there was, of course, the question of Yekaterina to consider.

So to avoid any confrontation—knowing full well that an exchange of words would benefit David, who in the eyes of his mother, if not in Yekaterina's, was held in far higher esteem— Alexander stepped forward and made to speak himself. But before any words could pass his lips, his mother pushed by him carrying a tray of tea and *kada*. David was quick to get to his feet and relieve her of her burden. As he set it down on the table, she patted him gently on the cheek.

"You are such a good boy, David Suliashvili," she said. "Your mother must be very proud of you."

David offered a brief bow. "All sons should try to make their mothers proud," he said and looked openly toward Iosif still standing propped against the mantelshelf. Then he took a pastry from the tray, popped it into his mouth, and chewing it said, "And I do not think I have ever tasted such wonderful *kada*. You must give me the recipe so I may pass it on to my own dear mama."

In the corner of the sitting room Alexander's father stirred in his chair. He had fallen asleep after dinner, but the commotion of tea and pastry had roused him. Seeing that his wife was pouring out strong black tea into tall samovars he grunted his dissent, then pulled himself from his deep chair and crossed to where his drinking horns hung from a peg on the wall beside an ikon of the Virgin. He took one down, found a bottle of wine on the sideboard and removed the cork.

"Koba," he said, his voice still gruff with sleep, "have some wine with me and leave the tea and cakes for the women."

Iosif offered his own semblance of a bow, an awkward and somewhat insufficient imitation of Dayid's, and replied, "I thank you, sir, but I must refuse. It muddles the senses."

Again Alexander's father grunted and proceeded to fill his horn with wine. He took a long drink, then wiped his lips with the back of his sleeve. "I do not trust a man who refuses a drink," he said, eyeing Iosif.

"Some people do not trust a man who takes one too easily."

It was Yekaterina who spoke, and all turned to look at her in the rocking chair, where she continued to embroider as if nothing had been said.

"And some insolent daughters deserve to be punished when they speak," said her father as he took a step toward her, his barrel chest thrust forth in indignation.

Iosif moved away from the mantelshelf, not so far as to bar the bigger man's path, but enough just to catch his attention. The room went very quiet, and there appeared now in the aspect of Alexander's father a pellicle of fear; it descended over his features like an early spring mist, growing thicker and more obscuring as Iosif spoke.

"I do not think Yekaterina meant you any disrespect," he said, his voice taking on a wintry tone. "I believe she only spoke of imbibers in general. There are those who lose their reason when they are in their cups. Not you, of course, sir, but others. Is that not what you meant, Yekaterina?"

Alexander looked to his sister, to the warmly appreciative and satisfied smile that touched her lips.

"Why yes, Iosif Vissarionovich," she said sweetly. "You have understood me well. As have you always."

Not liking the confidence that had just passed between her daughter and her son's shabby friend, Alexander's mother spoke up in a harsh voice.

"Tell me, Soso," she said, using the hated pet name that his own mother had called him by, "are we to understand that you are now an Ottoman?"

Iosif turned his dark eyes on her, but did not allow her taunt to upset the pleasure he had taken from Yekaterina's obvious affection.

"You might say," he replied, touching the top of his fez with his crooked left hand, "that this is my one concession to fashion. Besides, it is the headwear of our worker brothers to the west. When the revolution comes, it will spread well beyond Tsarist boundaries, and so we must be prepared with the foreknowledge of our comrades' ways. And how better to understand them than to walk in their clothes?"

"That is utter foolishness," said David, finding himself able now to release his frustration at being overlooked by Yekaterina.

"Really?" said Iosif with undisguised contempt. "I would have thought it the reason for your dressing like a bourgeois office clerk, so that you might know how better to cut them down when the time is ripe."

His words hung in the air like an implicit threat. Alexander moved quickly to diffuse the tension. He set his samovar back down on the tray and kissed his mother on the cheek.

"It was a lovely supper, Mama," he said. "But Koba and I must go now. We have much still to do this evening."

"More juvenile intrigue, I suppose," David said, though his voice now lacked all authority.

Iosif stepped close to him.

"It is only by virtue of our juvenile intrigue," he said through a hollow grin, "that thinkers like yourself, David Suliashvili, can claim any importance. You should not forget that."

Then Iosif executed a second bow, this one far more graceful than his first, and said, "I thank you all for your very kind hospitality."

———⁓⁓⁓———

Alexander waited in the shadows while Iosif spoke to the watchman in the guardhouse of the brickworks. After a moment his friend waved him over. The guard, drawing a large key from his ring, unlocked the gates and let them swing open for the two men. Iosif put a hand on Alexander's shoulder and ushered him through, saying, "Kamo and the others are already inside waiting for us. The tools have arrived."

They followed the watchman across the yard, past the brick kilns to the warehouse at the back of the works. There they saw light through the windows. Alexander noticed Iosif shaking his head at the sight of this, and then reaching out with his crooked hand to grab hold of the watchman's sleeve.

"Did you not tell them to be secretive?" he said, his voice clipped. "Do they not know that the Tsarists are watching out for us?"

"I told them so, Comrade Koba," the watchman said. He was a big man, thick through the shoulders with a great stone of a head, yet under Iosif's questioning he seemed almost to shrink in on himself. "But Simon Ter-Petrosyan . . . I mean Comrade Kamo, told me to mind my own business and showed me his pistol."

"Very well," said Iosif. "Lead on."

As they reached the door of the warehouse they could hear laughter coming from inside. The sound of the voices, along with the burning lights, served to worsen Iosif's mood. And although Alexander could not clearly see his friend's face in the darkness, he knew that it had hardened with fury. Iosif himself took hold of the door and flung it back on its rusting hinges. The light flooding out momentarily blinded Alexander, whose eyes had grown accustomed to the dark. But Iosif stepped into the glowing warehouse as if the new brightness had no effect on him.

"If I were the *gendarmerie*," he bellowed, "you would all be dead men."

Those inside stopped what they were doing and stared at the figure planted in the door frame.

"Simon Ter-Petrosyan," Iosif called out, eschewing the other man's party name in his flush of anger. "Come here at once."

From the back of the warehouse a young man came forward. He was tall and handsome, his dark hair framing his olive face, his dark eyes offering a warmth that was absent in Iosif's. He approached with almost sheepish steps, on his lips the shy smile of a child who knows he has been caught misbehaving.

"Koba," the young man said, drawing close and opening his arms. "I am so happy that you have at last arrived. Tell me, how did you find Yekaterina this evening?"

The words seemed to catch Iosif momentarily off his guard, and he hesitated; it was interruption enough for his anger to diminish.

"That's enough, Kamo," he said. "Do not try and change the subject. What is this with all of the lamps burning and the noise you are making? From outside, this place sounds like a reception hall. You know very well that the *gendarmerie* are trying to keep us under surveillance."

"Koba, Koba," Simon Ter-Petrosyan said, playfully putting his arm around Iosif's shoulder. "We took precautions. I have men outside keeping watch."

"I saw no men."

"You were not meant to," said Simon. "They are very good. They could slit a man's throat before he had the chance to feel the knife. Not yours, of course. They know the great Koba by sight." Simon turned to Alexander and winked. "But you, Alyosha," he said. "You will need to take more care. I am afraid they do not yet know your face."

Alexander did his best to share in the joke, but there was an undertone to it that disturbed him, a hint of warning that said Simon would not hesitate if such a thing were asked. The young man was devoted to Koba, and it was a devotion that caused in Alexander some concern—such fealty could prove dangerous.

"Enough banter," Iosif said. "Show me what we have."

"Yes, of course." Simon's eagerness was as childlike as had been his earlier humility. He led them to the rear of the warehouse where there stood parked two phaetons, their harnesses empty. On the floor between the buggies was a collection of crates. Simon knelt beside one and pulled back the loose packing straw to reveal a number of small grey metal cylinders. Iosif shrugged.

"They are new," said Simon with a catlike grin. "Comrade Krasin's latest noisemakers."

"But do they work, Kamo?"

"Oh, Koba, they do indeed. The raid last week in Batum. One alone killed two draw horses and a *gendarme*. It exploded beneath the carriage wheels and lifted it clear off the ground."

"Very good," said Iosif, nodding with approval. "And weapons?"

Simon lifted the lid of a second crate, longer and thinner than the first. Inside, fitted into wooden slats, were five factory-new Mosin-Nagant rifles. "We have enough for each man," he said. "And we have revolvers enough, as well. It is best that we have two guns each, in case anything goes wrong."

Iosif continued to nod. "Very good," he said. "Very good." Then he looked around the warehouse at the other men. They appeared tired and haggard, their clothes worn and their hair dirty—like proper workers. "Yes, Kamo," he said with approval. "I think it is all very good."

"But the best is still to come, Koba." Simon smiled. He turned then and reached beneath the seat of the nearest phaeton and withdrew a tunic. It was that of a Tsarist artillery officer, and was brushed clean and had polished buttons.

"Mikhail Ivanovich shall wear it," Simon explained. "His fiancée, Karolina, has agreed to ride alongside him. In the other phaeton will be Vasily Gregorovich, and he shall be accompanied by Mikhail Ivanovich's sister, Lidia. They will appear like nothing more than two lovesick couples courting in the summer's sun."

"You have outdone yourself, Kamo," Iosif said. "Tell me, though, where did you get the uniform?"

Simon lowered his eyes as if in apology and said, "Let me say only that the good officer no longer has need of it."

Then, reaching a hand inside the tunic, he poked his finger through a small hole just below the left breast pocket. When he did this, his eyes widened again and he gave a hearty laugh.

"Oh, yes, Kamo. Very good, indeed," said Iosif. "You do the revolution proud. Now, I shall let you finish your preparations, and then I would like to speak to the men."

Alexander followed Iosif to a table on the far side of the warehouse near a small window that looked out onto the yard. Sitting down, he watched his friend pack his straight black pipe with tobacco and light it, the sweet-smelling smoke cutting through the mustiness of the warehouse air. Iosif appeared pleased with himself. For a long while he blew lazy clouds of smoke toward the loose windowpanes, watching as the draft coming through the gaps in the frames curled the fumes.

"One day, Alyosha," Iosif said, as if he were talking to the tumbling smoke. "Mark my words, one day all of this will be over. The world will be put right and the people will no longer have to suffer the tyranny of fools. And I have a dream for when that day comes. It is a simple dream of a simple life. A small *dacha* in the mountains; a garden; maybe some goats. No more than I need, just enough to sustain me. I could be happy with that, Alyosha. In truth, I could be happy with less were I to know that Yekaterina would be at my side."

Alexander looked at his friend. At first, the thought of Iosif's dream of living the peasant life was laughable, if for nothing more than its wildly romantic inaccuracies. Then, too, there were the actualities: the notion of Iosif clad in coarse provincial clothing, squatting on a splintery stool, squeezing the sagging teats of a nanny goat. But there was also something in it that appealed to Alexander, and that was the idea of his sister's happiness. Unexpectedly he too fell victim to idyll: Yekaterina standing in the doorway of a gingerbread house, her face, so drawn of late, so hollow and so often without mirth, brightened by the mountain air and the happiness of being with the man she loved, even if she was too coy yet to give of herself fully, and her dark eyes alight with a joy she would never know in the home of her parents, gay and alive as she waited for Iosif to bring her the milk that she would churn into butter for their table.

"I wonder," Iosif began again, his tone unchanged, "if I should send one of Kamo's lookouts to pay a visit to David Suliashvili and his dear mama?"

—⁓—

The night caretaker let them in the stage door after Iosif gave a coded knock. It was daybreak, and they had been waiting in the alley that ran behind the Tiflis Theatre for almost an hour before Iosif approached the door. Inside, the caretaker led

them through the wings and into a back corridor with a staircase that climbed to the third-floor foyer. No one spoke. In
the foyer the caretaker left them; he disappeared back down
the staircase. Iosif went to a sofa beside the window and
looked out onto Erevan Square. It was empty in the half-light
of dawn, though Alexander knew that as the city awoke it
would grow busy with traffic. As he knew, too, that in three
hours' time the armoured government carriage would be
trundling across the cobbles with its cargo of bullion being
transported to the Tsar's treasury. And waiting for it would be
Kamo and his phaetons and his men.

Satisfied with their vantage point, Iosif settled back on the
sofa. It was upholstered in red velvet and had gilded legs
carved into the shape of bearpaws. He ran his hands over the
cushions. "What do you think of this, Alyosha?" he said,
caressing the material. "Do you think it is beautiful?"

"Some might think so," Alexander replied. He had never
been in the theatre before and was somewhat taken by its
opulence. Even in the dimness of morning, the deep burgundy
of the papered walls and the shimmering gilt of the fixtures
impressed him. This, he thought, must be what the Tsar's
palaces look like.

"The cost of this sofa alone," Iosif said, "could feed a worker
and his family for a year. What do you say to that?"

"I say that it is shameful," said Alexander.

"Yes, it is," said Iosif. "Come," he said, patting the cushion
beside him. "Sit down. See how the bourgeois treat their arses."

Alexander went to the sofa and sat down. He sank into the
stuffing; it felt to him like a great feather bed, and as he leaned
his head back, he was overcome with exhaustion. They had

been awake all night. When, some hours before, Simon had finished concealing Comrade Krasin's small bombs beneath the seats of the phaetons and distributed the guns and ammunition to his men, Iosif had given them their orders. His instructions were precise: where each man was to place himself around the square; at what position the armoured carriage was to be attacked; who was to throw the first bomb; who was to fire the first shot. Alexander was impressed by his attention to detail; every aspect of the raid was choreographed. Afterward, once each man involved had recounted to Iosif the part he was to play, Iosif told him to get some sleep before they had to start out. But Iosif himself was in no mood for sleep, and he'd kept Alexander awake with talk of Yekaterina. Now, with a sleepless night past and the welcoming comfort of the sofa pulling at him, Alexander felt himself beginning to drift toward slumber. Only the daunting insomnia of Iosif kept Alexander from surrendering himself.

"I have been thinking, Alyosha," Iosif said, shifting himself on the expensive cushions. "I believe I shall change my name."

Alexander sat up and looked at his friend. Iosif had changed his name many times in the past, assuming aliases to keep the authorities at arm's length. But it did not seem to Alexander that his friend was talking this time about an alias. There was an air of purpose about him now, as if this pronouncement was to be a declaration of presence, rather than a cloak of concealment.

"And what," Alexander asked, "were you thinking of changing you name to, Koba?"

Iosif smiled, and his face once again was that of a mischievous pixie. He leaned forward and in an exaggerated whisper said, "Man of Steel."

"Man of Steel?" said Alexander.

"Yes," his friend replied, puffing out his rather thin chest. "Man of Steel. What do you think?"

"I think it is a good name," said Alexander, though he wondered if Iosif might not be taking himself a little too seriously. "A strong name."

"And I am a strong man," Iosif retorted. "Am I not?"

"You are that, Koba. Everyone knows it to be true."

"Yes," said Iosif. He turned then and looked out again over Erevan Square. The sun had inched its way above the rooftops and shone brightly now through the window. "You should sleep now, Alyosha," he said, still peering down into the street. "You must be very tired."

"I am," said Alexander.

"Then sleep," Iosif said. "It will be hours yet before the carriage arrives. You want to be fresh when the action begins." He turned and smiled warmly. "Don't worry. I will wake you in plenty of time."

—〰—

Alexander felt a tap on his shoulder. He opened his eyes to the brilliant sunlight that flooded through the tall windows and bathed the foyer in a warm glow. Everything looked unreal to him and for a moment he thought he might still be dreaming. In his sleep he had been walking through an enormous ballroom crowded with people in evening dress who danced and spoke only to one another.

"It's time," Iosif said. "Kamo has sent the signal. The phaetons are on the side streets and the carriage is coming toward the square."

Alexander stood up and looked down at the busy pavement below. For some reason, he had not expected the square to be so crowded.

"Get away from the window, Alyosha," Iosif snapped. "We must not draw any attention to ourselves until it is time."

Iosif turned then and started toward the main staircase that led to the front lobby of the theatre. Alexander followed close on his heels. The steps were wide and shallow and covered in a deep red carpet the likes of which he had never before seen. It gave beneath his feet like the loam that covers a forest floor.

The lobby was empty. Iosif crossed to the front doors and disengaged the lock, then stepped behind a pillar so that any passersby could not see him through the floor-length windows that fronted the theatre. He motioned for Alexander to hide himself behind the pillar on the opposite side of the entrance.

Alexander could feel his heart racing. The rush of adrenalin lightened his head, and he found the sensation not at all unpleasant. It was similar to that which he had experienced as a child when his father took him into the hills to shoot rabbits. He looked across to Iosif, who was studying his pocket watch, his lips moving as if he was reading something written on the face of the timepiece; then Iosif returned the watch to his pocket and withdrew a revolver from the waistband of his trousers. Alexander did not recall him collecting a gun from the warehouse.

"Koba," he said. "Where did you get that from? I do not have a gun for myself."

"Do not worry," said Iosif. "Stay close to me and everything will be fine. And keep yourself behind the pillar and away from the glass."

Just as the last word passed Iosif's lips, Alexander heard a loud voice in the street outside. It was followed by a brief silence, but in that quiet moment it felt to Alexander as if the world were frozen in place: everything became still. Then came a clap, like thunder, and the great windows blew in and rained shards of glass through the lobby. Another clap followed and another close behind, much louder now, and then everything was quiet again. Except it was not. Alexander looked toward the other pillar and saw that Iosif was calling to him, though he could not hear a word his friend said. Iosif came and grabbed him by the arm.

"It is begun," he shouted.

Now the world came alive again and Alexander heard cries coming from the street as he allowed himself to be pulled through the front doors of the theatre.

In the square, the first thing he noticed was the smell: the stench of cordite and sulphur hung in the air and it brought to mind the thick perfume of incense burned during Easter Mass. After this came the bodies. They lay all around him: on the pavement, on the cobblestones; some were still, others twisted in pain, clutching at arms and legs, hands pressed to stomachs, chests. One old woman sat in the middle of the street, her skirts pulled up over her knees, the kerchief on her head stained red. She held her hands out to him as if begging for coins; her lips quivered but she made no noise. Alexander turned away from her and followed Iosif deeper into the square.

The phaetons had drawn up close to the armoured carriage, one at the back and the other in front, so as to block any route of escape. It was an unneeded precaution. The carriage was going nowhere. Of the two horses harnessed to it, one lay on its side, its belly torn open and its innards spilled onto the cobbles; the other remained standing in the reins, a rear hoof raised off the ground, tail flicking at its bloodied haunches as if to chase away flies. Kamo's men had swarmed the carriage and prised open its doors, and were in the process of removing the sacks of bullion.

Alexander stopped a moment and regarded the scene around him. It was as if there, in the centre of the square beside the carriage, he was in the eye of a terrible storm. All around chaos reigned. The horses of the Cossack Guard that had acted as escort circled the periphery of the square with empty saddles, like coursers at a steeplechase that had unseated their riders. And the remainder of Kamo's men had set upon the Cossacks themselves. Above the cries and confusion there came the sound of gunshots.

Alexander turned then to find Iosif. He saw him kneeling beside the carriage. Propped against the front wheel was the young soldier who, moments before, had driven the armoured carriage into Erevan Square, unaware of what awaited him. Iosif leaned in toward the soldier so that their heads were close together, as if they were sharing a confidence. Then he got back to his feet, placed the barrel of his revolver against the bridge of the soldier's nose and fired a bullet into the young man's skull.

Iosif slipped the revolver back into the waistband of his trousers and walked over to where Alexander stood, still staring at the dead soldier. He took him by the shoulder.

"Come, Alyosha," he said. "We must go before the gendarmerie arrive."

—⟨⟩—

They followed back streets and alleyways to the safe house, having at one point to hide themselves in the narrow confines of a doorway to avoid a *gendarmerie* patrol that passed on a nearby thoroughfare. They made sure to move quickly, but did not run, knowing that to do so would have drawn attention.

When they arrived, the old woman who kept the house, the mother of a local party member, was waiting for them with warm bowls of *chikhitma*. She also set out dark bread and a plate of cherries and currants. Iosif sat down at the table and tore off a chunk of bread; dipping it into his bowl, he began to eat with great fervour. But the smell of the mutton soup caused Alexander's stomach to turn; he thought of the horse with its belly laid open. So instead of the *chikhitma*, he took some currants from the plate and sucked on them, allowing their sourness to leach into his tongue.

"You are not hungry?" the woman asked.

"I do not have much of an appetite at the moment," Alexander apologized. "It is all the excitement, I think. Though I am sure it will return to me soon enough."

The old woman smiled, and in her face Alexander saw again the old woman from the square. He had to look away.

"You should eat, Alyosha," Iosif said. "It will settle your nerves."

"You are right, of course, Koba," Alexander replied and took up his spoon. It took more effort than he thought himself capable of to chew the greasy meat, and more still to swallow it.

Iosif, however, did not appear to suffer a lack of appetite; he ate like a man who had not seen food for days. Positioning his mouth close to his bowl, he spooned his soup with one hand and dipped his hard bread with the other. When he'd finished, he took a handful of currants from the plate and poured them into his mouth, sat back in his chair and released a satisfied belch. He then began to prepare a pipe.

It was a wonder to Alexander, this apparent detachment, this ability to carry on as normal after all that they had witnessed. He could not deny his envy of such composure.

Once his pipe was lit, Iosif set it between his teeth, stretched his arms out and brought his hands together behind his head.

"It is a good day, Alyosha," he said. "Today we have done a good thing."

"Yes," said Alexander somewhat uncertainly. "I suppose we have."

"Oh, there is no supposing, Alyosha. We have. It is a fact." Iosif sat forward in his chair again. He took the pipe from his mouth and pointed its stem at Alexander. "In fact, Alyosha, today is a doubly good day."

"Really, Koba?" said Alexander. "How so?"

"I have come to a decision, Ayosha," Iosif said and waited, his head tilted back slightly so that he gazed at Alexander down the length of his nose. It was something of a demanding posture, but Alexander could see in the faint wrinkles of his eyes that it was a pose and nothing more. Iosif was playing with him, so he agreed to play along.

"It is cruel to keep me in such suspense, Koba," he said, accepting his role with an actor's feigned distress. "I must know what it is that you have decided."

"You will be pleased," Iosif said.

"Not if I am kept in the dark," said Alexander. "In the dark I will be miserable."

"Then I shall bring you into the light," Iosif said, his tone becoming serious once more. He placed his pipe in his mouth and leaned forward with his elbows on his knees. "Alyosha," he said, "your dear sister, Yekaterina Svanidze, my darling Kato, is the only woman I will ever love. There is nothing in the world as dear to me as she. I cannot live without her. For without her, nothing matters. Without her there is nothing of worth in this world, not even human life. And I shall marry her, Alyosha. Yekaterina shall be my wife."

Alexander, hearing these words, recalled his vision of Yekaterina waiting happily in the doorway of her gingerbread house.

"But, Koba," he said. "You know how she feels."

"Yes, yes," said Iosif, pushing himself up again and waving his crooked hand. "She will only be married in the church, I know. But I tell you this, Alyosha, if that is what sweet Kato wants, then that is what she shall have. And I do not care a damn what the party has to say about it. Besides, was not Comrade Lenin himself married in the church? If he, then why not I? I said as much to the soldier in the square."

Alexander looked confused: "What do you mean, Koba?"

"Yes," said Iosif, "I know. You are her brother; I should have spoken to you first. But I only decided right at that moment. You must understand, Alyosha, I felt such joy, such absolute joyous certainty, that I had to tell someone. He was closest to hand. And do you know what he said to me, that foolish boy?"

"What, Koba?" said Alexander. "What was it that he said to you?"

"I'll tell you," replied Iosif, sitting back in his chair and crossing his arms over his chest. "He said, 'You are a pig.'"

Iosif was quiet for a moment, and Alexander could see his eyes darken.

"I told that Tsarist that he should not have said that to me. I breathed it into his ear like his mother when she whispered him to sleep. I told him that I was the Man of Steel, Stalin, and no longer a whore's son from Tiflis." Iosif thumped his withered hand against the arm of the chair. "And I told that useless stripling that my word was worth more gold than could be carried in one hundred armoured coaches, that it was worth more than the lives of one thousand jumped-up carriage drivers. Yes, Alyosha, that boy would have been wise to stay quiet. Now he no longer has the choice."

Alexander remembered how Iosif had leaned in close to the young man, how he'd cradled his head with one hand and pressed his lips to the soldier's ear and how he'd then put the bullet in his brain. "Yes, Koba," he said quietly.

Iosif's face broke into a grin again; his eyes brightened and he slapped his knee.

"So, what do you say to that then, Alyosha?" he said through his silly smirk. "We are to be brothers."

Alexander forced himself to smile: "I say it is the most wonderful news, Koba. I say that you will make Yekaterina very happy with it." But he was no longer so certain. It was as if a sliver of ice had worked its way into his belly and there settled in him a chill of uncertainty.

CASUALTIES

WHEN EDWARD OPENED HIS EYES AGAIN it felt as if a vise were clamped to his temples. He leaned forward and adjusted the vent on the dash so that the cool air-conditioned breeze blew straight into his face. The sheen of sweat began to slowly evaporate, leaving him with a chill. He reached for the can of Coca-Cola that he'd opened and left untouched in the cup holder before drifting off to sleep. It was warm and slightly tinny but he swallowed it greedily. The syrupy sweetness was welcome, but as the carbonation reached his stomach, he began to feel nauseated. He only spoke to hide his discomfort.

"Is this an autobahn?"

Paul responded without looking at him: "Autobahns are in Germany. We're in Belgium now."

Edward nodded, though it hurt him to do so, then turned and gazed out the passenger window toward the city that stood

143

some miles to the north. It sprawled hazily across the horizon, beyond the dry and dusty flatlands that shimmered in the midsummer heat, its outskirts obscured by a low-lying smog that was broken finally by stark high-rise buildings.

"What's that?" he asked.

"Brussels."

Edward felt as if he should say something more, but his hangover had too firm a grip on him. So he said nothing and leaned his aching head back against the headrest. The previous evening was little more than a blur to him now. There had been a great deal of laughter, he remembered that. And something had been broken; he was fairly certain that he'd done the breaking. And there'd been angry words between him and Paul, though he wasn't certain what about. It had been very late at that point and he was stretched out on the bed in the guest room. Possibly something about the woman, whose name was now well beyond his powers of recollection. Best let things alone, he decided, having learned long ago that drunken words are redressed at peril.

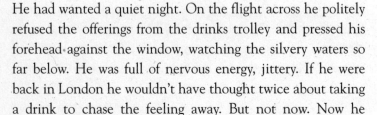

He had wanted a quiet night. On the flight across he politely refused the offerings from the drinks trolley and pressed his forehead against the window, watching the silvery waters so far below. He was full of nervous energy, jittery. If he were back in London he wouldn't have thought twice about taking a drink to chase the feeling away. But not now. Now he wanted a clear mind.

The airport at Maastricht was comforting. The Dutch, Edward noticed immediately, unlike the English, were not ones for clutter. And as he passed unchallenged through customs, it was like walking into an automobile showroom: all glossy polished floors and glass walls that looked out onto the passing traffic. Clean lines and smooth surfaces, the polar opposite of grubby, confused London.

Edward half-expected his brother to be in uniform. Not his utilities but his dress blues, complete with sharp creases, epaulettes, spit-polished boots and peaked cap. But Paul was wearing narrow-legged, faded blue jeans with a mauve golf shirt tucked in snugly at the waist. On his feet he wore a pair of new white trainers. Edward felt strangely disappointed.

They hugged awkwardly and Paul reached down and took up Edward's suitcase before he could protest, then led the way through automatic glass doors to a silver four-door Mercedes sedan in the parking lot outside.

"Whose is this?" Edward asked as Paul tossed the suitcase into the back seat of the car.

"Mine."

"Very nice."

"Don't be too impressed. They're dirt cheap over here."

A calm descended on Edward as they drove out of Maastricht and toward the German border. Only an hour's flight from London, and yet he had the sensation of having come home; this part of Europe held a distinctly Canadian flavour. The roads touched him first: excessively wide with gravel shoulders sloping away into shallow ditches. And then there were the fields that stretched out on either side after they'd passed into Germany—the only indication of the border now a subtle blue EU signpost. The crops of sugar beet, their stalks shifting in the breeze, were not hidden behind the tall privet hedges or stone walls of the English countryside, but openly displayed—a sea of deep green to bathe the eye. And as they reached Geilenkerchen and made their way along the sleepy residential streets to Friedlichstrasse, the cul-de-sac where Paul lived, Edward felt as if he were in the suburbia of his childhood. Large single-dwelling homes with proper paved driveways and closely trimmed weedless lawns, flower beds rather than planters, and cement walks leading to front doors with steps and screens. It made the cramped flats and narrow car-crowded streets of Kennington seem unnatural. In the parked Mercedes, looking at the scene around him, he imagined the past three years of his life in London fading away into nothing.

"Where's Sheila?" Edward asked after removing his shoes in the front hall.

"Home. Flew back a few days ago to visit her mother. Didn't I tell you?"

Paul hadn't told him, and Edward was sorry to hear that his sister-in-law was away. He'd hoped to have both of them there. He wanted to talk and had been counting on Sheila's level-headed perspective.

After he'd settled himself away in the guest room, and taken a quick walk through the house—which he found slightly cold now, even in the intense July heat—he found Paul reclining in a chaise longue on the concrete patio in the backyard. He accepted the cold can of Labatt's Blue out of nostalgia rather than thirst. The first crisp sip chased away the chill from indoors, and sitting down in a lawn chair opposite his brother, he was overcome by an intense feeling of familiarity.

"I've arranged a little get-together," Paul said, raising his can to Edward. "In your honour. What do you think of that?"

"Sounds great," Edward replied, hiding his disappointment.

People started arriving before they'd finished their first drink. They were fellow airmen, Québécois mostly. They came with their wives, some brought along their children and all brought cartons of Canadian beer and steaks and hamburgers picked up that day from the CANEX on the NATO base.

Despite his misgivings, Edward found himself enjoying the evening. The smell of the barbecue, the cold cans pressed upon him and the familiar accents from home acted as a balm, soothing away his uneasiness. The men were loud and back-slappingly friendly. They were proud and happy and more than once took Edward to the street out front of the house to show off their cars: Mercedes-Benzes and BMWs and Audis and a Porsche. Automobiles that they couldn't have dreamed of owning back home, but here, where luxury was domestic and the servicemen's salaries were inflated and tax free, there was the possibility of owning two. And back in the house, the wives pointed out Paul's dining-room table and chairs, obscenely solid oak, and the massive wall unit that held fine china and a carousel clock, and thrilled at the fact that they all owned the same, though some in blond; all bought on the cheap in Belgium. Back in Canada these same furnishings would cost the equivalent of the down payment on a bunga-low. In the backyard, which stretched down a grassy slope to a linked fence, Edward kicked a soccer ball with the children, breaking a sweat and falling twice, and calling himself Franz

Beckenbauer. It was a party and though he hadn't thought it possible, Edward was in a party mood. It was nothing like the dreadful, tight-lipped cocktail affairs Linda dragged him to back in London, but free and easy and unbounded.

It was late when the woman arrived. She was an officer and a hush descended when she stepped through the door. It was brief, but noticeable. Others coming in had been greeted with shouts and friendly gibes that Edward didn't understand, though he shared in the laughter that followed. But when she arrived conversations faltered, then were picked up again, their volume conspicuously raised, as if to make amends for the momentary lull.

She wore her uniform, with the sleeves of the blouse rolled tightly up her forearms. Paul went to her and shook her hand, then led her from the front hall and up the stairs. Before Edward had the chance to ask about her, he was swallowed up again in the conversation he'd been having with a lance corporal from Baie-Comeau. The next time he saw the woman, her standard-issue blouse was hidden beneath one of Paul's sweatshirts. Edward recognized the Roots logo; he'd given it to his brother for Christmas the previous year.

Did they argue about the sweatshirt, Edward wondered; it was entirely possible considering the state he was in. Or maybe it was the lamp. That's what got broken, he now recalled. It had sat on an end table beside the sofa, and when Edward flopped himself down on the cushions his elbow struck the shade and toppled it to the floor. He laughed when it smashed against the tiles because the lance corporal did, and he felt a bond had grown between him and the Frenchman. One of the airmen's wives swept up the mess, and Edward had the vaguest recollection of having made a comment, something disparaging, about her buttocks, which sent the lance corporal into another shuddering bout of laughter.

He wished now that he hadn't drunk so much. He wished he wasn't in the stifling car speeding along an autobahn, or not an autobahn, or whatever it was they called a highway over here. He wished he knew why Paul was so angry. There were a lot of things he wished.

"It looks a bit like Toronto, don't you think?" he said, his head still lolling against the headrest.

"What's that?" Paul said, staring straight ahead.

"Brussels."

"Sure. I guess so."

Edward turned and looked back at the city as it faded in the distance. He could feel his stomach begin to turn.

"Do you miss it at all?" he asked over his shoulder, then looked at his brother. "I mean Toronto? Home?"

Paul turned his head partway toward him.

"Not a bit."

• II •

His plans had all gone to pieces, like the ceramic table lamp his brother had smashed the night before.

The fields that encircled Geilenkerchen were to have been the starting point, the first instalment in his historical monologue that would take them out of the Westphalian countryside and along the Rhine to the bridge at Nijmegen, then down into the heart of Belgium and east until they reached the cemeteries of Ypres. But Edward, ruined from the previous night, had fallen asleep before they'd even reached the outskirts of the town.

It was here, Paul wanted to explain, in the seemingly endless flat stretches of sugar beet, that the Americans had faced some of the fiercest resistance during the final push for Berlin. The Battle of Geilenkerchen was a bloody affair. To take the town, they had first to cross these terrible fields, which would have looked much the same then as they did now: peaceful swelling carpets of green. But as the Yanks sent wave after wave of riflemen into the breeze-rippled pastures, they were cut down by Wehrmacht machine guns hidden in the tall grasses. The bullets tore low through the sugar-beet stalks. It took three days to capture the fields, whose midsts were criss-crossed with shallow trenches that concealed the German guns. By the time the Americans gained the town, it was as if the earth itself had been bludgeoned.

From Geilenkerchen he drove north toward Düsseldorf and the autobahn that would take them along the eastern bank of the Rhine and on into the Netherlands. He crossed the river first at Kleve so as to come at the city of Nijmegen from the north, via Arnhem. This was to have been a lesson in perspective. They would make the leisurely trip from sleepy Arnhem to Nijmegen inside of thirty minutes, whereas it had proved a nearly impossible trek some fifty years earlier. Of the British paratroopers who had made it to Arnhem, only one in four emerged unharmed. Those unlucky enough to reach the bridge at Nijmegen melted under the searing hail of German fire and could go no farther. Paul had wanted to shake his brother awake as they crossed back over the Rhine and tell him that this was the same bridge from the movie, but did not.

Sitting there behind the wheel, fiddling now and again with the volume on the car stereo in the hope it would disturb Edward's slumber, he felt himself growing angry. He desperately wanted to build up to what he had to tell his brother— to, in a manner of speaking, soften the target. Yet even with the opportunities of Geilenkerchen, Arnhem and Nijmegen missed, Paul decided family lore might be enough to serve his purpose. This final story he would save until they had passed Brussels and headed into the Belgian province of West Flanders. Edward would recognize it as soon as Paul began the telling. In fact, Paul was counting on it. It would be best if they told it together, shared the narrative.

It had been a Remembrance Day tradition. Every eleventh of November their father would sit them down on the floor in front of his chair and tell them the story of what had happened to his father's father in the Great War. Pappy Dan, as their father called him, had been a soldier in the trenches. And when they asked him what a trench was he explained that it was like a big ditch, deep enough that no one could see you even if you stood straight up. He told them too about the mud and the rats and the lice and how when the soldiers' feet got wet they got trench foot, which meant that their feet went black and smelled like rotting meat and sometimes their toes fell off. He made certain that his sons understood just how terrible war could be. How sometimes the armies bombed each other for so long that grown men curled up in tight little balls and cried like small babies. And how there was a place called no man's land where if you fell down and couldn't get up again you were left to die. And there was a gas called mustard that if you breathed it in would make you drown even though you weren't anywhere close to water. Paul remembered that for the longest time Edward wouldn't put mustard on anything, not bologna sandwiches, not hot dogs, nothing, because he was afraid he might die. And after telling them all this their father would go on to say how one day, in the middle of a bright summer's afternoon, Pappy Dan's captain ordered them all to climb over the top of the trench and run out into no man's land toward where the Krauts were, even though there were bombs falling out of the sky like rain and so many bullets flying about that they made the air sizzle. The army said, he told his boys, that one of those bombs that was raining down fell right on Pappy Dan, and that when the smoke finally cleared, he was gone, blown away into nothing. All that was left was one boot: the right one. It didn't matter how often they'd heard the story, whenever it reached this point, both Paul and Edward grew so anxious that they could no longer remain settled. Their father would always pause here, waiting for his sons to calm, then he would smile. Of course, he would continue, that wasn't what *really* happened. After the war one of Pappy Dan's army buddies found Pappy Dan's brother and told him the truth about Pappy Dan. He hadn't died at all, hadn't been vaporized in the stinking sticky mud of no man's land. In fact, the only part of Pappy Dan that had even been on the battlefield that day was his right boot, carried out and left on the foul dirt beside a bomb crater by a pal who, as misfortune would have it, never made it back to the trenches himself. As for Pappy Dan, having had a bad feeling about the next day's attack, he'd sneaked away in the night, in the company of a Flemish farm girl he'd become smitten with, and made for France, slipping past the sentries, one foot booted, the other bare, determined to live to be an old, old man, just him and his plump little peasant maiden.

Edward shifted slightly in the seat beside him and let out a low groan. He raised his hand sleepily to his temple, then let it fall again into his lap.

"I hope it hurts," Paul said quietly.

• III •

Edward turned the map over in his hands, trying to decipher it. The mass of criss-crossing coloured lines marking highways, country roads, rail lines and rivers, along with the confusingly foreign names, some in French, others in Flemish, made no sense to him. Edward had no idea where they were. He could see where they'd come from, and could put his finger on their destination, but their whereabouts in the mass of squiggles in between was a mystery.

"Here, I think," he said to Paul, holding the map toward him and pointing a finger. "Oudenaarde. Didn't we just pass a place called Oudenaarde?"

"Not that I saw," his brother replied.

"Oh." Edward looked at the map again. "Well, maybe not, then."

Paul had handed the map over reluctantly when he'd offered to help navigate the remainder of the way to Ypres. And Edward had made the offer only because he'd felt guilty for having slept through the better part of the journey. He knew this trip was important to his brother. All things military had fascinated Paul ever since they were young. In particular, he had been taken by the stories their father told them, many of which, Edward later realized, had been gleaned from the old black-and-white movies he watched on late-night television. Paul knew this as well, but he'd never let it dampen his enthusiasm.

And so, when he'd phoned the week before to ask if he might come over for a visit, just to get out of London for a few days, and Paul suggested they make the car trip to the many battlefields that crowded this small corner of Europe, he'd feigned excitement, if only to make his brother happy.

He looked at the map again. They were supposed to be making a detour to a monument dedicated to the Second Battalion Princess Patricia's Canadian Light Infantry that Paul had heard about from one of the guys in his unit. Paul had made the decision on impulse, something he was not prone to doing, and Edward was happy to act as his guide. The monument was located outside a small village called Zottegem, and although he could see the site clearly on the map, a tiny red maple leaf marking the location of the memorial, there was nothing in the sprawling farmland they drove through that appeared remotely like a town, small or otherwise.

It was his fault, Edward knew, that they'd lost their way. He hadn't been paying attention since they'd turned off the two-lane highway and onto the bumpy country road. He'd done his best to concentrate on the map, but soon found that although the car was winding its way through the hinterlands of Belgium, his head was back in London. It was the map. Its chaotic intersections of spidery lines reminded him of the legend for the Underground. That in turn reminded him of Linda, and he wondered just how many times his wife had ridden the Northern Line toward Edgware before he'd finally summoned the courage to follow her.

—⚡—

Edward had his suspicions. Never anything definite or concrete, just awkward, intangible feelings that would come upon him unawares, when he was in a meeting with clients discussing a new campaign, or sitting in front of his computer banging out more bland copy for Anglia Rail or Tescos. Sometimes it was a fluttering in his stomach, sometimes a loosening of his bowels, sometimes a constriction in his chest; sometimes it was all of these together. And he would have to lean back if he was sitting, or sit if he was standing, and take a slow deep breath and fight the urge to grab the nearest telephone and call home. The telephone calls only made him feel worse, waiting with the receiver pressed close to his ear while the short double rings went unheeded until the answerphone finally picked up and her voice taunted him: "You've reached 5-7-4-5; neither Edward nor Linda are available to take your call. Leave a message at the tone and we'll ring you as soon as we're able."

He would always hang up before the machine beeped; then chide himself for having made the call in the first place. For once having done so, the rest of his day was ruined. His concentration compromised, he would spend his remaining hours at the office imagining horrible things of his wife.

Once, returning home to find Linda curled up on the settee in the lounge watching the evening news, he'd asked where she'd been, said that he'd called her from work. She'd smiled sweetly and said, "I did pop out to the shops for a bit. You must have missed me then." He hadn't bothered to tell her that he'd been phoning all afternoon.

When the day came, he steeled himself with vodka in his breakfast orange juice. Three quick glasses while Linda was in the shower. He waited until he heard her turn off the faucets, then called down the corridor to say he was leaving. She opened the bathroom door.

"Drop in at the cleaners on your way home and pick up my black dress, will you," she said, her hair bound tightly in a white towel, another wrapped around her body, cinched across her breasts. "I want to wear it to the Wooltons' tonight."

Seeing her there, framed in the lingering mist of the shower, Edward wanted to cry, to lie down on the floor and weep, and have her hold him and rock him against her chest. But he just smiled stupidly and promised not to forget.

After leaving the flat, Edward went to a caff on Kennington Park Road, ordered a cup of tea and took a table two in from the window and waited. Half an hour later he saw her walk by. She was wearing loose cotton slacks and an oversized T-shirt that fluttered at her waist. Her hair was down and slightly frizzy, which meant she had used the blow-dryer. From her shoulder hung the woven and beaded tote bag he'd bought for her the year before on their trip to Morocco, the one she used to carry her supplies: notebooks, pens, Tipp-Ex, mini-tape recorder; and her sundries: mints, tissues, debit card, lipstick, tampons.

When she was well down the street he slipped out of the caff. He followed at a distance, keeping constant the space that separated them. She slowed outside a chemist's, as if collecting her thoughts, then continued on. At the Kennington tube station, Edward lingered on the pavement, waiting as she purchased her travel card from the automated wicket, then he followed suit. Again on the platform he had to lag back, this time pausing in the tunnel as she sat on a bench and searched through her bag. When the train arrived he waited until she'd boarded before he slipped into the car directly behind.

It being past the rush hour, the train was close to empty, so Edward took the seat nearest the coupling and watched her through the window, ready to tip his head back behind the frame should she look in his direction. He needn't have worried. Once seated, she pulled out a paperback novel and was immediately engrossed in her reading. Seeing her and not being seen, Edward found himself growing excited. In her ignorance at being watched she took on a natural innocence. He imagined her a stranger on a train with whom he could fall completely and instantly in love. Then he remembered what he was doing and the twisting feeling of sickness in his belly returned.

To fight the fluttering nausea, he thought about the world carrying on above: the bustle of Charing Cross; the tourists in Leicester Square taking pictures of the lions and feeding the diseased flocks of pigeons; the chaotic hub of Euston Station; the jabbering markets of Camden Town.

Preoccupied with these musings, he'd almost missed her leaving the train at Belsize Park. When he'd glanced through the window and seen the empty seat, he'd panicked and jumped up, making it through the sliding doors just as they were about to close. Coming around a corner in the tunnel, he had to stop short and step back out of view, not having realized that the station had lifts rather than escalators. He waited until the few people gathered there had got into the elevator and were on their way to street level before he pressed the button for the second car. It seemed to take forever to arrive and he became frightened, sure that he would lose her in the wasted moments.

Outside the station, he almost walked straight into the back of her. She'd stopped at a flower stall and was smelling carnations. He stood frozen only a few feet behind her.

"Fresh cut this morning, miss," the flower seller said. "Shall I wrap a dozen up for you?"

"Thank you, no," she replied, and Edward could tell from her voice that she was smiling. "Though they are lovely."

Then the flower seller caught Edward's eye and was about to ask him the same, so he turned quickly away and walked a short distance in the opposite direction. When he turned back, he saw that she had started up Haverstock Hill toward Hampstead. He trailed behind her again, trying to re-establish the distance he'd settled into on Kennington Park Road.

This part of London seemed a world away from where they lived; the bistros and cafés and boutiques that lined the wide sidewalks were almost intimidating in their affluence. The wrought-iron chairs in the roped-off, umbrellaed patios and the darkened interiors of the upscale shops seemed designed to exclude rather than invite. And as Edward passed them he felt as if eyes were turning in his direction, aware and accusing.

As Haverstock Hill became Rosslyn Hill, the *ristorantes* and shops gave way to great Victorian townhouses, their front gardens closed in by thick stone walls. Those few that had been converted into flats were ragged and peeling, and looked embarrassingly apologetic. But the others stood indignant in their rectitude, their polished and gleaming panes glowering down at Edward as he passed by.

She stopped before one of these and hitched up the bag on her shoulder before pushing through the iron gate, which swung smooth and silent on its hinges.

Two doors away, Edward stood behind a wall that was topped with shards of green glass. He watched as she rang the bell and bounced nervously on the balls of her feet. The door to the house opened almost immediately and a man stepped onto the threshold. Even from a distance Edward could see that he was tall and well built, a dusting of grey silvering his temples. His face was clean-shaven and pinkish, and he wore beige corduroy trousers and a soft burgundy pullover. He had his hands in his pockets.

They stood there looking at one another, unheard words passing awkwardly between them. Edward felt the lightness of relief. A freelance job, he thought. She must have picked up an interview for one of those glossy magazines she'd done some writing for.

He'd just been considering what a fool he'd been when they pulled one another close and kissed so hungrily, so passionately, there on the front step for all to see, that Edward felt as if he'd been kicked—a violent, heavy boot in the softness of his belly. And then they were gone, swallowed up by the house, the door closed tight behind them.

Suddenly, it was as if everything he knew had been taken from him. He was a stranger, lost in a foreign city with no map to guide him.

He ran all the way back to the tube station but couldn't bring himself to re-enter. He couldn't do it, couldn't sit on that train again as it snaked its way under the city and back to their home. He hailed a black cab instead and sat doubled over in the wide back seat all the way to Kennington. He had the driver drop him outside a pub a few streets away from their flat. It was a rough-looking place, not the posh local that he and Linda met their friends at on Thursday nights. He sat there alone at a table drinking pints of thick stout until half-past two. Then he went back to the flat. He needed to sleep, but the thought of climbing into their bed made him feel sick. So he curled up on the settee, closed his eyes and waited for his wife to return. When she shook him awake at a quarter to five, he told her that he'd been taken ill, that he'd come home early from work. He apologized for not picking up her dress.

• IV •

It should have been simple enough: four turns, easily identifiable on the map, and they would find the plaque on a large stone by the roadside. Or so the master corporal from the airframe shop had told him. But there was nothing but scrub pasture and wire fencing as far as the eye could see. And Edward didn't seem at all bothered by it. So Paul pulled the car onto the shoulder and stopped.

"Just give it to me, will you," he said, trying to keep his anger in check.

His brother handed him the map and by way of apology offered a meek shrug of his shoulders.

Paul spread the map out against the steering wheel and traced with his finger the route they were supposed to have taken from the main highway. Two kilometres down the first road they were to have taken a right, which they had. After another kilometre, a left, followed by a second left, half a klick on. That was where they made their mistake. There were two roads set very close together that ran parallel to one another for a short distance before veering gently in opposite directions.

"Which of these did we take?" he asked Edward.

His brother leaned toward him and looked at the map. "What do you mean, which?"

"I mean, which," Paul said, feeling his throat begin to tighten. "Did we take the first road or the second?"

"I'm not sure."

"Well, there you go then," he said, and refolded the map. He looked at his watch. It was getting on past two in the afternoon and he wanted to be at Ypres by four so they could be back on the road home while there was still plenty of daylight. "Let's just skip it," he said, "and get back on the highway."

"Look, I'm sorry, all right," Edward said, a slight catch in his voice. "You didn't say anything about there being two roads."

"Don't worry about it," he replied as soothingly as he could. "I'm sure it wasn't much to look at anyway."

Below the marker, Paul knew, were the remains of fourteen engineers. They lay there, under nine metres of dirt, entombed when their tunnel had caved in on them. All had been volunteers, their mission to burrow their way under no man's land to the enemy lines so as to open another avenue of attack. Aware of the plan, the Germans had shelled the ground above, collapsing the cold earthen roof and burying them alive. Paul had wanted to read and remember their names.

After they'd turned around and were heading back along their misread path, Paul let his eyes wander across the rustic countryside. He could see now what Edward was talking about when they passed by the outskirts of Brussels. There was something in this landscape that was recognizable, reminiscent of Canada. What came to mind, as he gazed out across the fallow acreage, were the wide, flat reaches of farmland outside Port Elgin, where Sheila's parents lived. She would be there now, probably just waking up in the bedroom that was still decorated with stuffed animals and pretty-boy posters, just as it had been when she moved away to go to college in the city. She would be pulling on her pink terry-cloth robe and sliding her feet into her oversized fuzzy slippers and heading down the wide wooden staircase to make herself a strong cup of coffee. Or maybe she would still be buried beneath the comforter on her bed, crying.

She will have told her parents by now, Paul thought, her mother at least. How would she react, he wondered. She was a good woman, always kind to him, always genuinely warm. Whereas Sheila's father had been standoffish. A quiet, sturdy farmer, he never showed emotion: neither disapproving nor affable. It felt strange, realizing that he was now utterly cut off from them. He had hurt their child, had become the enemy.

Next he thought of his own mother. She would be devastated. She'd grown so close to Sheila during the years of their marriage. He recalled how her face had lit up when he'd announced their engagement. They'd been sitting out back of the house, on the wide cedar deck he'd spent all summer helping his father build the year before he enlisted. His mother had put her hands to her face, as if to hold back tears.

"A daughter," she said. "Finally, after all these years in a house full of men, I'm getting a daughter."

There'd only been he and Edward, and their solidarity had always lain with their father. It was as if with Sheila's arrival his mother had gained a long-awaited ally, the much-needed reinforcements that allowed her to assert herself in what had been a dominion of men. She took strength from her daughter-in-law and used it to support herself. Together they were more like sisters. And now he'd destroyed that as well.

He dreaded the prospect of having to explain himself. What would she say? he wondered. There was no gentle way to relay what he had done. No way to tell it where he didn't end up sounding the villain. Would it turn her against him? How couldn't it? How could his mother not hate him for stealing Sheila away from her?

He would have to make her understand that what he was doing was the right thing. That it made him happy. And wouldn't she want him to be happy? It would have been easier of course if he could lay the blame on Sheila. If he could say to his mother, "Look what she's done to me." But she had done nothing. She'd simply carried on unaware as he set about dismantling the world they'd built together. In bed at night she curled against his turned body, fitting her knees perfectly into the hollows of his own, and inhaled the scent of his freshly showered body.

"You're using a new soap," she said once. "I like it."

It had been so easy to hide it from her. Already in the habit of showering after his rotation, washing off the grease and dust of the hangar, it took little effort to deceive her when it was Jenny's smell he began to wash away.

Finally, he could no longer carry on with the lies. Deception was too untidy, and he'd begun to pity Sheila. And this made him feel as if he was betraying Jenny. So in the end, even afraid as he was of the gossip that would surely follow in its wake, he told her the truth.

Sheila's reaction shocked him, left him cold. He had expected her to crumple, had imagined that she would fall to the floor in front of him, or shatter like the fragile china she had so loved to collect and put on display for all to see. But she did neither.

She stood with arms folded tightly across her chest. She had just finished cleaning the kitchen and the dishtowel dangled from a closed fist. All around her, ceramic and stainless steel shone. She did not speak, and all Paul could think of was how when they first arrived at the house there had been nothing in this room except pipe fittings and electrical outlets, the previous tenants, as was customary, having taken their kitchen with them: counters, cupboards, appliances, fixtures, everything. Sheila had taken care of the refit. She chose the cabinets, decided on Italian ceramic for the counter tiles, high-polished faucets and the double sink, matching refrigerator and stove and dishwasher. The kitchen belonged to her and her alone.

"It's not that I don't love you anymore," he said to her, hoping that this would somehow shake her from her silence.

"I do love you. I do. It's just . . ." And he could think of nothing to add.

She walked to the sink and, after wiping away a last drop of moisture from the edge of the basin, carefully folded the towel and laid it on the cool counter tile. Then she turned to face him.

"You will book me on a flight home tomorrow. I don't care what you tell them. Say my mother is ill."

The calmness in her voice frightened him.

"Of course," he said. "Whatever you want."

"Really?" she asked. "Whatever I want?"

"Yes," he replied, unsure of how he could ever manage to keep his word to her again.

"Then what I really want is for you to fall down dead right here in front of me." She smiled queerly at him. "Do you think you could manage that?"

· V ·

After driving through the unexceptional town of Ypres, they thought they'd lost their way again. The cemetery was supposed to be on the outskirts, just off the highway heading south. But there was nothing other than low-slung red-brick houses crowding the edge of the road. Ten kilometres out of the town centre, Paul pulled onto the gravel shoulder and studied the map closely. Then he turned the car around and headed back toward Ypres, slowing again as the town came into view.

It was Edward who saw the sign, small and green with white lettering. It bore the Canadian War Cemeteries emblem and

stood at the entrance to a dusty laneway that passed between
two of the nondescript red-brick houses and ended abruptly at
a low metal barrier. Beyond the barrier stood the cemetery,
enclosed by a short sandstone wall.

They gained entrance through an opening in the wall
and once inside stood there, not knowing what to do. To
their left, from behind a tall juniper hedge that bordered the
cemetery, they could hear the voices of children playing in
the backyard of one of the houses. To the right was a vast
and rolling meadow, its tall grasses shifting in the warm
summer breeze. In the distance stood a copse of trees, elms
maybe, possibly oak—they were too far away for Edward to
tell. It was an idyllic view that stood at odds with this
strange little graveyard that, although its grasses were neatly
trimmed, felt somehow neglected, shut out of view by hedges
and walls and houses.

"This isn't what I expected," Paul said, looking around him.
It seemed insufficient, did not jibe with the picture he had
in his mind. He'd prepared himself for something grand. The
previous November he'd been part of the colour guard at
Normandy, representing the Canadian servicemen who'd
fallen during the D-Day landings. Before the ceremony he
walked along Juno Beach in the cold spray blowing off the
Channel, wondering at the horror those men must have felt as
they ran across the loose, shifting stones at the water's edge.
And then, inland, he marvelled at the vast cemetery
stretches, row upon row of white markers ranging out in all
directions like some sort of gruesome harvest. He'd been
gripped by conflicting emotions: awe and pride and sadness.
Yet none of these feelings were intimate. The magnitude of

loss, the efficiency of death, the solemnity of sacrifice was too overwhelming to be visceral. But here, in this wanting, misshapen plot of land, he felt as if a cold hand had reached into his chest and touched his beating heart.

"Did you think it would be like this?" he asked his brother.

Edward shook his head. He'd been thinking about poppies and the lines of McCrae's poem, about failing hands and rows of crosses. But there were no crosses here, just stark white headstones with maple leaves etched into their crowns, all but indistinguishable from one another. And there was no order to their placement, no symmetry to the layout. The rows were staggered, some running perpendicular to others; in some places stones were bunched together in small groups, while in others there was empty grass; at the far end, one headstone stood alone. The cemetery had a hurried look about it, as if there hadn't been time to worry about the economy of space, as if burial had been a nuisance.

—⚲—

There were seventy-eight headstones in the cemetery. Edward had counted them, touching the top of each one, before he went and sat down on the wall and looked out over the open field. At first he'd read the names on the markers, but soon found that he was taking in only the dates of their deaths. Of the seventy-eight, sixty-three had perished on the same day: the fourteenth of August 1917. Gas, he thought, and the taste of mustard filled his mouth.

Behind him, Paul moved slowly through the graves, stopping for a moment at each one and every so often bending down to run his finger over the engravings.

Edward tried to imagine the land before him torn and broken the way he'd seen in the picture book his father used to show him when he was a boy, but he couldn't. Those photographs had been black and white, grainy, water marked. They might as well have been of the moon they were so alien to what he looked at now. It was quiet and green and sweet smelling.

"I can't see it," he said to Paul without turning.

"What's that?"

"All the terrible things. It must have been a nightmare here, worse than anything imaginable. The gas would have drifted across like a cloud come down to earth. They would have seen it coming. But I can't." He shifted himself to look back at his brother. "Can you?"

Paul closed his eyes and let the breeze play against his face. He shook his head: "It wasn't gas. Not here, not then. Artillery, more than likely; or they were making a push across no man's land." He turned back to the tombstones, reading each as if looking for one name in particular.

This place wasn't peaceful, Edward decided. Sedate maybe, but not peaceful. Nowhere that was ever so violent could be that. It was at rest, out of its misery. He heard the children laughing again and felt a chill. Paul came up beside him and leaned against the wall, facing the opposite direction.

"He's not here," Paul said quietly. "He should be, but he isn't."

"Who isn't?" Edward asked.

"Pappy Dan."

"Did you think he would be?"

Paul nodded. "I did, yes. This was his company. At least that's what it said on his induction papers. I found them, you know. A couple of years ago, in the archives at the War Museum in Ottawa. They've got all that stuff there. Packed away in cardboard file boxes."

"You never told me about that."

Paul shrugged. "I didn't think you'd be interested."

"I might have been."

"You might've."

"Did you really want him to be here?" Edward asked.

"Not at first, no," Paul said. "But now that we're here, I guess I do—or at least part of me does."

Edward stood up and stepped back over the wall. He crossed his arms and rubbed his shoulders as if he was cold, then walked to the closest marker.

"I'm glad he's not," he said as he bent down and picked up a pebble from the grass and laid it on top of the gravestone.

"It was a good story, though," Paul said, his voice somewhat uncertain. "Wasn't it?" Then he started walking again, down each row, his gaze passing from stone to stone.

Edward, watching as his brother marched through the dead ranks, could feel his heart beginning to spill. The look on Paul's face was that of a lost child searching for a familiar landmark that would show him safely home. He waited as Paul made another circuit of the cemetery, waited until he drew the map from his back pocket and spread it across the top of the low stone wall, then he went and stood beside him.

Paul lifted his head and looked across the field.

"There's another one over there," he said to Edward. "Maybe we should check it out."

Edward smiled. "Or we could just leave it be," he said. "It was a good story."

"You think?" Paul asked.

"Parts of it were," said Edward. "Him running away with that farm girl. You know, just lighting out and starting all over again." He reached out and took the map. "I liked that bit."

"Yeah," said Paul as he watched Edward carefully refold the map and slip it into his shirt pocket. "I liked that bit, too." He could feel his body go lax then, as if he'd somehow come untethered, and looking out across the field, he was overcome by a sense of foreignness. He was no longer certain where it was that he belonged. Then he felt Edward's arm around his shoulder.

"Come on, Paul," he heard him say, as if from very far away. "Let's go home."

THE TIME BEFORE

TRY AS HE MIGHT, Elizaphan Misago could not get used to the cold. There was no escaping it. It chilled him to the jellied marrow. No matter how many layers he wrapped himself in or buried himself under, winter's sharp finger still pricked through, penetrating skin, muscle and sinew until it needled his very bones.

Standing behind the Plexiglas wall of a bus shelter that offered little refuge from the February wind, he thought of how warm it must be in Tallahassee, Florida, where his son lived. His son who refused to take him in; refused the sponsorship the American government required before they would issue him a visa. He recalled how the consular official in Bukavu had casually shrugged his shoulders when he broke the news.

"I'm sorry. We've been in contact, but he refuses to act as guarantor. Without that, there's nothing I can do. It's out of my hands."

And as if to show that help was truly beyond his grasp, the embassy man held up his hands, fingers splayed, palms open.

Elizaphan had thought momentarily of a bribe, but knew he had nothing to offer. All he'd once owned was gone, abandoned when he fled across the border. His home, his car, even his medical practice belonged to others now; others who, no doubt, had stripped everything as cleanly as a dog would a corpse.

"You might consider Canada," the American had said, a slow smile creasing his fleshy, sunburnt face. "They're far more amenable to refugee claimants. And with your professional standing, I'm sure you won't have much difficulty."

Had he known about the cold and the reluctance to accept foreign credentials, Elizaphan might have thought twice about his choice of country. He might have risked Belgium or even gone back to France where he had studied as a young man; at least there they were up front about not wanting you.

Still, even after the college of physicians had denied him accreditation—that he'd studied at the Faculté de Médecine de Nantes did not matter; to them he was still an African doctor—Elizaphan felt there were benefits to Canada, and Toronto in particular. Other of his countrymen, he knew, would gravitate toward Montreal or Quebec City, language being their succour. Which was why Elizaphan chose differently. He did not wish any such comfort, nor did he wish the chance of old acquaintance. He wanted to avoid reminders of the past.

Geography, though, Elizaphan had discovered, could be as feeble as will when it came to combatting memory. He'd learned that lesson shortly after his arrival in the city. It came some weeks after his caseworker found him the apartment overtop the transmission shop on Ossington Avenue. A cramped, lifeless set of rooms with narrow casement windows high on the walls that admitted very little light. The stink of motor oil, grease and exhaust fumes from the garage below made the air close.

"This will not do," his caseworker said. She was a short, plump woman with waxy skin and a forced smile. She had taken him gently by the elbow and tried to coax him back toward the stairwell. "Come, doctor," she said. "I'm sure we can find you something better than this."

But Elizaphan stood his ground. He was determined not to return to the holding centre in the hotel beside the airport. Even with its comfortable beds, private baths and colour television, it reminded him of the camp in Zaire. He would sooner live in a dungeon than go back there. So he smiled and, in the overly polite, overly gracious, overly submissive manner that he'd come to recognize as the obligatory conduct of the refugee, assured her that the apartment would be fine.

Elizaphan took to walking to escape the smell and the headaches it brought him. At night, with the shop below closed and the windows of his apartment open, the air was breathable. But during the day he had to flee out of doors. At first, he explored the immediate neighbourhood, the residential streets that ran between Bloor and College, and those that slipped across Harbord and bordered the park at Christie Pits. It was late summer then and the sun was still strong. He found work washing dishes at a Greek diner on Clinton Street. His caseworker had suggested that he enrol in one of the city's adult learning centres to improve his English. It might help for when he decided to sit the examinations required by the college of physicians. But Elizaphan thought less of medicine. It too belonged to the past.

Instead he concentrated on becoming lost in the city: a nameless face in the multitude, insignificant in his existence. He preferred the crowded streets, where it was easier to go unnoticed and to be unnoticing. Pushed along by the tide.

Then came a Sunday morning in late October. He found himself stopped on the sidewalk out front of St Michael's Cathedral. It was unseasonably warm; an Indian summer, the cook at the diner had told him the previous afternoon. It took Elizaphan a moment to realize what it was that had halted his progress. In consideration of the mild weather, two of the cathedral's doors had been left open, and through them drifted the sweet voice of the choir. Elizaphan, who'd served as an altar boy in his youth, recognized the processional hymn sere- nading the congregation as they made their way to receive the Eucharist. He stood and listened, but did not feel the urge to enter. Elizaphan had not been to church since before Zaire, even though there had been many priests in the camp and Mass was said often.

He walked on, heading west toward Yonge Street, before the parishioners emerged. Still, the sound of the choir and the unexpected brilliance of the sun had served to lighten his mood, and for the first time since his arrival, Elizaphan felt a sensation akin to belonging. He moved along the sidewalks as if he were weightless, bouncing on the balls of his feet. And without realizing it, he'd begun to look at the faces of those he passed by, taking unconscious pleasure in the fact that when he met an eye he did not feel the immediate need to look away.

At Dundas, Elizaphan crossed the street and began to make his way toward the entrance of the Eaton Centre. He was happily weaving through the mob of shoppers and tourists and street kids and panhandlers, softly humming the hymn he'd just heard. When he saw the face, the song caught in his throat, stuck like a stone in his windpipe. It was there ahead of him, motionless in the shifting throng, staring out at him. The features were immediately recognizable: the high forehead and long cheeks, the tapered chin, the thin nose and lips, the skin slightly less dark than his own. Eliel Nkongoli. But Elizaphan knew it was not Eliel. Knew that it could not be Eliel. For he had seen the man's body himself, had stood over it and looked down upon the head split open by a machete, flies feeding in the wound.

Elizaphan ran. Ran from the face that could not be Eliel Nkongoli's, though the resemblance was enough almost to make him weep. A taxicab screeched its brakes as he stepped blindly into the busy roadway, the driver cursing him in a language he could not understand. Elizaphan continued running, pushing his way through the crowded Sunday sidewalks, not knowing where he was going, his mind awash with horrible images: Eliel, his wife and two daughters, seven and nine, their bodies lying bloody and torn in the foyer of the hospital.

—∽∽—

At night Elizaphan dreamed of the time before. When his wife, Agathe, was still with him and his son wrote loving letters and sent photographs of his happy family in Tallahassee, Florida. It was as if he were able to summon specific images and replay them in his dreams like home movies. They flickered through his slumber in brilliant Technicolor, but were devoid of sound. The one he called upon most often was his and Agathe's last anniversary, and the trip they'd taken together to Kigali.

They stayed at the Hôtel des Mille Collines in an executive suite with their own private balcony, but spent most of their time at the poolside or wandering through the hotel's extravagant gardens. In his dream he did not recall the long trip from Kibuye or the disheartening drive through the slums northeast of the city, only their time together at the hotel.

Some nights were filled with meticulous renderings of their anniversary dinner at Le Panorama, the Hôtel des Mille Collines' top-floor restaurant. A small candlelit table against the window, where they looked out onto the distant purple silhouette of Mount Mikeno in the setting sun. He and Agathe began with *escargot de Bourgogne*. Garlic butter dripped down her chin, making her skin glisten; Elizaphan wiped it away with his thumb. Later it was chateaubriand for him, *confit de canard* for Agathe. Dessert was *bavarois au cassis* shared between them. They finished a bottle of wine and two *café crèmes* before going downstairs to Stan's Bar, to drink cocktails and dance to music that was far too young for them.

There was also the afternoon they played tennis with the middle-aged couple from England. The man was in frozen-food storage and this was a second honeymoon of sorts. His wife, he explained, wanted to see the mountain gorillas, the ones Dian Fossey had found, but they'd been warned away from the area by the travel bureau. Agathe spoke far better English than he did, and on the court there was more conversation than play, which seemed to please the Englishman's wife, who showed little interest in the game. Afterward, they shared lunch and drinks at the Pool Bar, before the Britons set off to explore the city.

In his dreams their time was carefree: leisure without concern. It was only as morning approached that trepidation invaded. It appeared as a dimming in Agathe's eyes, as if a cloud had settled over her, blocking out the sun. At which point, as if a deaf man miraculously cured, Elizaphan was flooded with voices. But they were neither his nor Agathe's, nor those of the other hotel guests. Rather, they were the rabid utterances of Radio Television Libres des Mille Collines, warning all who listened that blood would soon be spilled.

Elizaphan took a seat in the rear of the bus. Below his feet, a discarded newspaper lay bloated in the melting slush. Already he'd become disenchanted with winter's snow. When the first flakes had drifted through November's sky, he'd stood on the sidewalk out front of his apartment and gazed upward in amazement. The mechanics from the transmission shop came out of the garage and laughed at him in a good-natured way. But when December brought the first ground-covering blanket, they paid no attention as he ran his fingers along the pavement and touched them to his lips. Now Elizaphan saw the snow for what it was: an impediment, turning the city salty and grey, disrupting it at whim.

He leaned his head against the window, the pane cold against his skin. The snowploughs that had run throughout the night had blocked in cars parked along the roadside. Here and there hurried commuters worked at digging out their automobiles, the vapour of their breath disappearing quickly in the wind. It was still early, but even when the sun finally climbed into the sky, there would be only a hint of its presence above the slate-grey clouds. It was like an angry hand, Elizaphan thought, pushing an icy pillow down over their faces.

He returned his gaze to the interior of the bus and began to count the passengers. Including himself, there were seventeen people. This was something he found himself doing more often now. Whenever he was in an enclosed space, he counted the bodies and tried to calculate how much room they would take up if they were piled close together.

The first time it had happened was at the diner. He'd just carried a tray of clean cups and saucers to the counter at the front, and as he turned to go back to the kitchen, he stopped and let his eyes roam quickly over the dining room. Thirty-six was the number he'd come up with. Add to that the three waitresses, two cooks, the manager and himself: forty-three. With all the tables and chairs removed it would take less than half the diner to accommodate them. Of this he was certain. For Elizaphan had seen far more bodies pushed into an even smaller area than that. Indeed, there had been more in the reception room back in Kibuye.

—⟩⟩⟩—

Eliel Nkongoli, whose face he now saw everywhere, had, like Elizaphan's son, gone to America to study medicine. But unlike Elizaphan's son, Eliel had returned to Kibuye.

Returned, taken a wife, begun a family and accepted a post at l'Hôpital Murengoru. A pediatrician, he was well liked by both his patients and the hospital staff. He was quick to smile and, it always seemed, even quicker to laugh. Elizaphan liked to imagine that his own son had grown into a man like Eliel, though he knew that it was probably not the case. His and Agathe's only child had always been a sullen boy, caring but rather downcast.

There was nothing downcast about Eliel. Quite the opposite. He was gregarious, fun loving. A quality he brought back with him from America. Many was the time that he invited the hospital staff, and not just the doctors, but the nurses and custodians as well, to his house overlooking Lake Kivu to eat and drink and dance late into the night. He called them his Yankee Barbecues. Agathe always refused to go, and forbade Elizaphan from accepting the invitations. She did not approve of Eliel's kind.

But Elizaphan admired him, if from a brief distance. For he also recognized the danger in such a man. Eliel Nkongoli, at times, spoke too freely and put too much trust in supposed friendships. Elizaphan could see in the eyes of his co-workers what Eliel could not. Behind their smiles and laughter was the old stain of resentment. And when, one afternoon, while sharing a coffee in the doctors' lounge, the young pediatrician expressed his ambitions—"You watch, Dr Misago, one day I will be prefect of Kibuye. Then, my friend, you will see things change"—it was as if a hand had reached out and put a mark upon his forehead.

Elizaphan rang the bell, deciding to walk the rest of the way. The bus had grown crowded and he no longer wished to count the bodies.

On the sidewalk, Elizaphan stood for a moment, letting the wind bite at his face. He looked around. The size of the city still overwhelmed him. A sprawling web that knew no bounds. And here, near the financial heart of the metropolis, the buildings ascended like glass mountains into the mean sky, their gold and silver mirrored panes reflecting the displeasure of above. Only once before had he been in a city of such immensity: Paris, when he was a medical student. But in many ways not even Paris measured up to the audacity of Toronto. Paris was a hive, restricted by its history and culture. Toronto was far too young, too naive to know such restrictions. And Kigali, Kibuye—they were stunted by things far more horrible.

He began to walk, careful not to slip on the ice beneath his feet. He took cautious, mincing steps, his arms held out slightly from his sides to keep his balance. And as he did so, he thought of the rain and the mud and that first camp at Bwakira. And of Agathe.

The rebels came, as everyone knew they would. To empty out the camp, they said, to send people home. The rains came with them, turning the ground treacherous. One minute it was like greedy hands clutching at feet and legs, the next like water on a marble floor. Behind the high walls of the central compound, the peacekeepers hid from the rain, and from the soldiers on the outside, who tightened the fences until those inside could no longer move, just sink into the quagmire. On the second day, those near to the gates were pulled through, kicked and beaten and told to return to their homes. On the third, the soldiers started shooting and the panic erupted. The peacekeepers barricaded themselves. The fences began to fall. The soldiers threw hand grenades and fired their machine guns into the throng. People ran madly, screaming, crying, trying to find the holes in the wire. Those that fell were trampled down and swallowed by the mud. Agathe let go of Elizaphan's hand, slipped to the ground. And he watched as she disappeared into the earth, before he turned and fled.

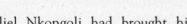

Eliel Nkongoli had brought his wife and daughters to Elizaphan's house. They followed a route that took them along the shores of Lake Kivu, thus avoiding the checkpoints that had been set up on the roadways. Elizaphan was standing in his kitchen, listening to the RTLM radio announcer warning everyone to stay in their homes. The president was dead and curfews were in effect across the entire country. He could hear Agathe crying in the lounge. It was then that he saw first one, and then another child being pushed over the wall and into his back garden. Then came Eliel's wife, followed by Eliel himself. He was not smiling.

Elizaphan turned off the radio and went out into the yard. It was a beautiful spring day, the sky high, blue and cloudless. A slight breeze came in from the lake and the scent of the bougainvillea Agathe so carefully tended sweetened the air. The only hint of anything wrong was the fear in Eliel's eyes. He gathered his daughters close to him and waited for Elizaphan to speak. But it was Mrs Nkongoli who spoke first.

"Dr Misago," she said, her voice clear and matter-of-fact. "Will you help us?"

Before Elizaphan had the chance to answer, Agathe appeared on the doorstep. Her eyes were red but dry, and when she spoke, it was in a tone that chilled the warm spring air.

"Send those cockroaches away," she said. "They deserve what is coming."

———✺———

When Elizaphan turned onto Bond Street the wind all but disappeared. He no longer felt its touch, but its voice sounded in his ears, like that of the ocean in a shell: an echo of the past.

As he walked, he glanced up at St Michael's Hospital, an enormous facility encompassing an entire city block. The sight of it made l'Hôpital Murengoru, and its three cinderblock storeys, seem insignificant by comparison. He paused a moment, having caught sight of two doctors casually chatting in the entranceway. One, a clipboard held against his chest, was leaning against a door frame laughing at something the other had said. And in that moment, Elizaphan found himself back in Kibuye, walking Eliel and his family past the *Interahamwe* barricade and on into the foyer of the hospital.

The corridors of l'Hôpital Murengoru were crowded with people, many of whom Elizaphan did not recognize. In among them he saw the faces of patients he had once treated, but when he met their terrified eyes they quickly looked away. He led Eliel down the main corridor and up the stairs to his own office on the second floor. This too he found occupied by strangers. He shooed them out into the hallway and told the Nkongolis to remain there, and not open the door to anyone.

At this, Eliel's youngest daughter began to cry, so Elizaphan rooted through the drawers of his desk to find the packet of sweets he kept as a special treat for himself. He gave one to each of the girls and handed the remainder over to Mrs Nkongoli. Then he made to leave, but she took hold of his arm before he passed through the door.

"You will come back for us, Dr Misago," she said.

Elizaphan looked to Eliel, who offered him but a weak semblance of his customary smile.

"Of course, Mrs Nkongoli," Elizaphan said. "I will see what this is all about and then I shall return. I promise."

Outside, the mob at the barricade had grown. Among them now Elizaphan saw familiar faces. Doctors and nurses, all of whom had shared food and laughter with Eliel Nkongoli at his Yankee Barbecues. They stood side by side with the bare-chested, machete-wielding young men of the *Interahamwe*.

One, a nurse, still wearing her pale blue uniform, and who had helped Eliel to run his fledgling pediatric wing, came up to Elizaphan and placed her hand gently on his forearm.

"Thank you so much, doctor," she said in a happy voice.

"For what?" asked Elizaphan.

She looked at him and laughed: "Why for bringing the cockroaches to us. Now we don't have go ferret them out."

A second young nurse came over then and stood beside Elizaphan.

"Yes, Dr Misago," she said, her smile mirroring that of the first. "And as soon as the prefect arrives we can be rid of them for good."

—⁓—

The steps leading to the doors of the cathedral were already cleared of snow and coarse salt had been laid down to prevent them from icing over. Elizaphan bent down and retrieved a large granule, then touched it to the tip of his tongue. As he held it there, it began to burn.

After the prefect arrived at l'Hôpital Murengoru, he'd stood on the hood of a truck and given a rousing speech, brandishing a pistol in one hand, and in the other a *masu*. He brought with him other armed men, who formed a protective phalanx around the truck. With each denunciation, the crowd cheered, thrusting their arms into the air, displaying to the sky the machetes and clubs and hammers and stones clenched in their fists. There was an air of festivity and the anticipation of mad feasting. Near the front, two nuns, their pressed hands raised aloft, began to sing. A celebratory hymn soon taken up by others. As the crowd began to surge forward through the gates and into the courtyard of the hospital, Elizaphan slipped away, the hymn still playing in his ears.

The door of the cathedral opened and a young priest, a novice to look at him, stepped out into the cold morning. Seeing him, Elizaphan pushed the rock of salt to the back of his tongue and swallowed it. The priest smiled and started down the stairs. He lifted the hem of his cassock so as not to stain it with salt. When he reached the bottom, Elizaphan saw that he had a wide, innocent face, his cheeks already rosy from the chill. On his chin there was a small razor nick, a tiny patch of scabbed blood.

"The start of a lovely day," he said, offering a short, sarcastic laugh. "Have you come for early Mass?"

Elizaphan did not respond.

The priest looked at his watch. "It'll be starting in about twenty minutes. You're welcome to come in now, if you like. Get yourself out of the cold."

"I helped to bury them, Father," Elizaphan said flatly.

"I beg your pardon?" replied the priest.

"We put them in a big hole behind the hospital. Threw dirt on their faces."

Now the young priest looked nervous. He regarded Elizaphan warily, then cast a quick glance up the steps.

"If you want," he said, extending a hand to Elizaphan, but withdrawing it before he reached his arm, "we can talk. I could hear your confession."

"No," Elizaphan said. "I have nothing to confess to you."

He turned away then, leaving the priest to stand alone in the cruel morning, and started back along the street, toward the sound of the wind.

SANT'AGNELLO AT DAWN

IT WAS HER IDEA to rent the scooters. She decided on the ferry across, thought it would add a touch of adventure. But the young man in the rental shop shook his head before they'd even finished asking. "Too dangerous," he said. And when his wife started to argue the point, Stanley Lesser quietly slipped out the door again. He walked partway down the hill to where the road turned back on itself and sat on the low stone wall that overlooked Marina Grande. It would be best, he decided, to let her talk herself out. As for the young man, Stanley was certain that he'd had to deal with Shirley's type before; he would be able to handle himself.

The guidebook had described Marina Grande as a lively little port with colourful fishing boats and quaint shops and *ristorantes*, the perfect jumping-off point to visit the rest of the island, but looking down on it, Stanley could see only the bustle. Maybe, he thought, it was the harsh August sun that had bleached away the colour and the charm. He hadn't imagined it could be so hot, near forty degrees even with the sea breeze. He felt uncomfortably sweaty, and his shirt, the white linen one Shirley had bought for him at Harry Rosen before they left, was wrinkled and sticking to his back. He was glad at least that he'd stood firm about wearing his Bermuda shorts, rather than the matching linen trousers. Shirley said, when she came out of the washroom and saw him wearing them, that he looked too much like a tourist. Stanley had resisted the urge to tell her that they *were* tourists; it wouldn't have mattered what they wore.

It was a foolish idea, really: scooters at their age. Stanley had turned sixty-one in May, and Shirley was three years his senior, though to look at them one would think it the reverse, and might indeed imagine the years separating them greater. For Stanley was thin and wispy, and had found a little of the stoop his own father had at his age, while Shirley was still buxom and dyed her hair cornsilk yellow and wore sheer cotton blouses and gold lace sandals. She liked heavy rings on her fingers and dark lipstick, and the idea that riding scooters across Capri might actually be a little dangerous. "If you're not living," she always said, "then you might as well already be dead."

Stanley's first wife was dead. Eight years now, though at times it seemed much longer, and at others not near so long. Shirley's husband had died, as well, but only two years before. And he had been her second husband; the first she divorced after a year.

Stanley and Shirley had met at, of all places, a mixer. A weekend getaway for lonely widows and widowers, though it wasn't billed as such. It had been called, if Stanley remembered correctly, the Survivors' Club—playing rather clumsily on the appeal of a popular television program. He went at the behest of his children, who felt that he had become too isolated. He needed to meet people. He argued that he was happy on his own, but they didn't believe him. So to allay their concern, and because the reservation had been given as a Christmas gift, he agreed to attend.

The weekend was held at the Sheraton Hotel and Casino in Niagara Falls, and when Stanley checked in he was met by the organizer, a plump young red-headed woman who beamed at him as one who's never known loss. She pinned a laminated name tag to his lapel after finding his name on the list. After she'd pressed upon him a dun-coloured portfolio with the Survivors' Club emblem on its cover and explained all the wonderful activities that were planned, he excused himself and made his way to the elevator. He had no intention of participating. And rather than attending the "Wine and Cheese Meet & Greet" and the "Getting to Know One Another Banquet Dinner," he settled down in his room to watch the cable sports station he did not get at home. At half-past ten and feeling like he might enjoy something other than what was on offer in the mini-bar in his room, he went down to the lounge. It was there that Shirley found him.

"You must be Stanley Lesser," she said, tapping him on the shoulder.

"Yes," Stanley said after a moment. "How did you know?" He had left his name tag in his room.

Shirley smiled and pulled out the stool next to him.

"Do you mind?"

"Not at all," Stanley said and watched as she settled herself primly on the seat, smoothing her dress beneath her. "Well?" he asked.

"Buy me a drink and I'll tell you," she said.

"Tell me and I'll buy you a drink," he said.

"You were meant to be sitting next to me," said Shirley.

"I am sitting next to you."

"Not here. At dinner."

"Oh."

"Yes. It was the only empty place in the entire room. I checked." She gave him a look of counterfeit annoyance. "You stood me up; I hope you realize that. For that alone you owe me a drink."

"Fair enough," Stanley said and motioned for the bartender. "You'll have to forgive me," he said, turning back to her. "It's just that I don't hold much with these sort of things."

"Really? This is my third one."

Afterward, they went to his room. And when Stanley woke up the next morning with Shirley beside him, the thought of going back to Toronto and his empty house didn't seem as appealing as it had the previous afternoon.

—— ∽∽∽ ——

Stanley Lesser's first wife was named Gloria, and they were married on a bitterly cold February day in 1962 at a small church in the town of Uxbridge, where he'd found a position with the local high school. The church no longer existed, at least no longer existed as a church. It had been disestablished and sold off to private owners who turned it into a gallery for local crafts people. He went to visit it the summer after Gloria died, and when he told the gallery director why he'd come, the man tried to sell him a ceramic vase.

He and Shirley were married at Fantasia Farms, a venue in the Riverdale valley that catered specifically to those who wished for something other than a church wedding. They had both already gone that route, Shirley reasoned, and why shouldn't they do something a little out of the ordinary? There were gardens and fountains, and statues of wood nymphs and gnomes, and the rumour of wildlife in the trees. Their vows were exchanged under a trellis on one side of a shallow fabricated pond that held varicoloured goldfish, while their guests stood watching from the other side. Then it was into a low-ceilinged, dark-panelled ballroom with a glass wall that looked out onto a stone terrace for the reception dinner. They kissed to clinking glasses, and afterward tables were cleared away for dancing. His children seemed pleased for him, if not altogether happy. Shirley did not have children of her own, but did have many nieces and nephews. One, a young man about the age of Stanley's son, drank far too much and tipped over a table of drinks before someone took him outside to get some much-needed fresh air. They saw him there, asleep on a patio chair, when they slipped away near the end of the night.

The hard soles of her sandals clicked on the pavement as she made her way back down the roadway toward Marina Grande. Stanley lagged behind. At the bottom of the hill she stopped and waited for him, her hands on her hips.

"You might have at least stayed in there with me," she said accusingly.

"I didn't really see the point," Stanley offered with a sigh. "He'd already made up his mind."

"Do you want to know what that man did after you left?" She paused as if to let the implications of her question sink in. "He pretended he couldn't speak English, that's what he did. Shrugged his bloody shoulders and said, '*Non capisco, signora.*'"

Stanley had to suppress the urge to shrug his own shoulders. There was, he knew, little that he could say that would satisfy her, so he said nothing. It was better to suffer her stare than provoke her with the wrong words.

"Well, I'll tell you right now," she said, jerking her thumb toward the queue of orange buses near the seawall opposite. "I'm sure as hell not taking one of those."

On this point Stanley was in full agreement. There was almost nothing as unpleasant as riding on a local bus. They'd learned their lesson the day before when they'd caught the orange bus from their hotel to the Piazza Tasso in Sorrento. Not only was it unbearably crowded, but there were no seats to speak of; all the passengers had to stand. And twice Stanley had fallen against the stern-faced conductor when the driver swerved to avoid oncoming traffic.

"We can always take the funicular," Stanley suggested.

He had actually been looking forward to taking the strange railway-cum-cable-car contraption after having seen pictures of it in the brochures at their hotel. But he could tell by the look on Shirley's face that this was not the answer she was after.

"No," she said matter-of-factly. "We'll take one of those." She pointed toward the taxi rank beside the hydrofoil-ticket kiosk, then started in its direction without waiting for his reply.

—⟶⟵—

It was their honeymoon, but they didn't like to call it that; instead, they called it their *trip*.

Shirley explained this to the couple across the coach aisle while Stanley leaned his head against the window and feigned sleep.

"We were actually married four months ago," Shirley said and patted his hand.

She was talking, Stanley realized, to cheer herself up. It had been a difficult flight, an overly long charter with a two-hour stopover at Exeter to collect an English tour group. After claiming the baggage from the carousel at the airport in Naples they'd had to find their assigned coach. Somehow Stanley had managed to get them on the wrong one. Discovering his mistake, he had to rummage through the cargo well for their suitcases, an annoyance to both Shirley and the coach driver, who stood by, his eyes shielded by dark glasses, refusing to render assistance. When they did find their own coach, Stanley had to stow the luggage, again without the aid of the driver. Then the only vacant seats were at the rear, and by that time Shirley was already hot and tired, so that the added discomfort of having to make their way down the narrow aisle put her in an even worse mood.

"Our hotel is called the Mercato," he heard Shirley say. "It's supposed to be quite lovely. Do you know it?"

"I've heard of it, yes," the man across the aisle said. "On the small side. One of those family-run places, if I'm not mistaken. In Sant'Agnello."

He could feel Shirley stiffen beside him.

"Really? We were made to understand that it was in Sorrento."

"All pretty much the same now," the man said. He and his wife came yearly to the Sorrentine Peninsula. "At one time they were separate villages: Meta, Piano di Sorrento, Sant'Agnello. Still, it's an easy walk into Sorrento proper; or you can always catch the orange bus."

"I see," Shirley said. "And where are you staying?"

"Us, we're at the Excelsior. It's on Piazza Teatro Tasso. Gorgeous spot. Overlooking the sea. Ibsen once lived there, you know."

"Well," Shirley said, "that does sound nice."

When the tour group representative, who'd been indifferently pointing out the sights during the hour-and-a-half drive from the airport, called out for the Mercato, Stanley and Shirley were the only ones to answer. She hurried them along, and the driver, who had simply stopped the coach in the middle of the busy roadway, retrieved their suitcases from the luggage compartment and dropped them rudely on the sidewalk.

Stanley looked around. "Where's the hotel?" he asked the representative as she climbed back aboard the coach.

"Oh, it's just around the corner and down a bit."

"And what about our bags?" Shirley demanded.

The representative, a freckle-faced and fair-haired Irish girl of no more than twenty, offered a sweet, well-rehearsed smile.

"It's really not so far," she said. "I'm sure you can manage." And with a hiss, the door of the coach swung closed.

At the Mercato, which was indeed *on the small side*, though quaint in its smallness, if a little tired looking, they found that their room was not yet ready. It was still being cleaned, the proprietor explained. He was a frail man with a bruised complexion who wore dark trousers and shirt sleeves that showed a vest beneath. He invited them to have a drink in the bar, and Stanley and Shirley followed as he led them to a small well-lighted room off the lobby. It was a pleasant little space, Stanley thought: narrow, with a cool marble floor and tall French windows that opened onto the cobbled side street. He had a tall glass of cold beer. Shirley had white wine, but she found it bitter and didn't like that the chairs they sat on were plastic.

—⚉—

The taxi dropped them in the Piazza Vittorio in Anacapri and the driver told them that he would be back in an hour to pick them up and take them to see the Faraglioni. Stanley didn't like the manner in which the man pointed at his watch as he spoke, as if the concept of time might be foreign to them. But Shirley laughed and placed a hand on the driver's arm and said, "Don't you worry, Antonio, we'll be here. On the dot."

She had flirted with him the entire drive, but Stanley had taken little notice. He'd been more concerned with watching the road. It wound its way precariously up from the port, skirting the boxy whitewashed houses that hemmed it in on both sides, making every bend a blind one that hid oncoming traffic from view until the very last moment. Coming around one such bend, Antonio—he'd introduced himself even before Stanley and Shirley climbed into the taxi—had to quickly jump onto the brakes to stop them from crashing headlong into one of the dreaded orange buses. The disaster averted, the next few minutes were taken up with Antonio and the bus driver arguing over which of them should give way to the other. In the end, the bus driver simply put his vehicle into gear and began moving forward, necessitating a quick reverse on Antonio's part. But he gave only enough room so that mere inches afforded passage.

From there it was onto the twisting two-lane blacktop that hugged the cliffside to Anacapri. All that separated their little open-air taxi from a sheer drop to the rocky coastline below was a flimsy-looking green metal railing—like the banister on a stairwell, Stanley thought. Just glancing out his side of the car caused him palpitations. It didn't help matters that Antonio spent more effort turned round talking to Shirley than he did on navigating the narrow slip of asphalt.

"Did you hear that?" she said at one point, slapping Stanley's arm to get his attention. "Antonio's driven Robert De Niro. And others besides, haven't you, Antonio?"

"Yes," Antonio shouted, turning almost completely in his seat so that he could look directly at Stanley. "Many. I have driven many."

"I wish you would keep your eyes on the road," Stanley said as politely as his fear would allow him.

"Oh, don't be silly," Shirley said, slapping him again. "He knows these roads like the back of his hand. Don't you, Antonio?"

"Yes," said Antonio, shooting Stanley a sly grin. "Like the back of my hand." And he swerved the car ever so slightly toward the guardrail and Stanley dug his fingers deeper into the upholstery.

—⟲⟲—

The evening before they'd had dinner at the Mercato. Stanley said that, as it was included in the package, they should at least give it a try. He didn't tell Shirley that the real reason they were eating at the hotel was that he felt obligated. The previous night, when he'd been waiting downstairs in the bar for Shirley to finish getting ready, the landlord had asked if they would be in for dinner. When Stanley told the man that they thought they might try O'Parrucchiano, a place that had caught Shirley's eye, he looked downcast.

"Yes," he said rather sulkily. "It is very good. Very nice."

"Tomorrow," Stanley said. "Tomorrow we will eat here."

At this the landlord brightened. "Good, good," he smiled. "Tomorrow."

He seemed happier still when Stanley and Shirley walked into the dining room the next night; it was as if they had kept a promise he'd expected to be broken. He met them at the door and showed them to a table by an open window. A soft breeze billowed the curtains, which the landlord made a fuss about tying back, before hurrying off to fetch a bottle of wine.

The dining room was large and airy, and the tables, covered with white linen, were placed in such a way as to afford intimacy without being obviously separated from one another. The walls were hung with crude pastel renderings of the fishing villages that dotted the Sorrentine Peninsula. They lent a homespun atmosphere to the place. The serving staff, who moved between the half-occupied tables and chatted with the guests as they portioned out the green salad and pasta from large metal bowls, reinforced this impression. Stanley found that he much preferred this to O'Parrucchiano and its ill-mannered waiters, even if the fare was somewhat less appetizing.

It was just after their salad plates had been cleared away that the elderly couple approached their table.

"Would you mind awfully much," the man said as he pulled out a chair, "if we joined you?"

The question appeared rhetorical, seeing as the woman was seated before Stanley had a chance to reply.

"We do so like to meet new people on our trips," the man stated as he took a chair for himself. "I'm Reginald Hopkins, but please call me Reg. And this," he performed a brief but gallant sweep of his hand, "is my wife, Domenica."

Stanley handled their own introductions rather awkwardly, and then sat in awe as Domenica called over the landlord and spoke to him in Italian, in a way that Stanley thought to be unnecessarily brusque.

"Is there something wrong?" he asked her after the landlord went away.

"Nothing at all," Reginald answered in his wife's place. "Just want to make certain we're not getting yesterday's stale pasta. You must ask, you know. Giuseppe's a lovely man, but he will try to pass off the leftovers for economy's sake."

There were a few uncomfortable moments at the start, the familiarity of the new arrivals catching Stanley and Shirley off their guard. But things soon settled down and Stanley found that he enjoyed their company. Shirley was quiet for the most part, nodding politely as their dinner companions chattered away. They had met and married, Reginald explained, during the war, when he served as an orderly with the British 10th Field Surgical Unit at Castellamare di Stabia. After the war, he'd studied medicine at Nottingham, before he and Domenica settled in Oxford, opening a practice that he'd retired from only two years earlier. "Eighty-one," Domenica said, only the faintest trace of her Italian accent showing itself, "and still he put up a fuss."

With coffee the talk turned to the local interests.

"The Amalfi Drive is, of course, something to behold," Reginald said. "There is, for my money, nothing that compares to it in beauty."

"We've booked ourselves on the tour for the day after tomorrow," Shirley offered, making her first real effort to join the conversation.

"No, no," Reginald said, shaking his head. "A coach is not the way to do it, I'm afraid. All herded together like sheep, watching everything through tinted glass. No, you must rent a car so that you can take your time. So that you can stop where *you* want to, rather than where they tell you. Cash in your tickets, my dear."

"They're non-refundable." Stanley shrugged.

"Ah, now that is too bad," Reginald replied. "Still, what you want to do to make amends is get yourselves on the ferry and visit Naples. Bloody marvellous place, that is."

"Oh, but it's full of thieves," Shirley said. "Every guidebook says so."

Now Domenica spoke: "I'm Neapolitan," she said flatly.

A lull fell over the table, and Stanley felt uncomfortable again.

"Of course it is true," Domenica said, breaking the uncomfortable silence, her voice all sweetness. "But then one can find horrible people most anywhere."

Anacapri was quiet, most of the shops closed for lunch. They wandered about the narrow streets, talking, when they did, in hushed tones as if in a church or a library. It was such a peaceful place, Stanley thought, and decided he preferred it to Sorrento, which seemed to be chaotic at every hour. But Shirley found it boring.

"It's like a ghost town," she said and suggested they have a drink before going back to find their taxi.

It took some searching, but they found a little café on a small street that led off of Piazza San Nicola. It wasn't much to speak of, just a few tables and an awning. The table they took had dirty cups on it and Stanley had to shoo away the flies. When the waiter finally came outside, Stanley ordered two *caffè americano* and watched as the man, the front of his apron stained, shifted the empty cups to another table. After the coffee was delivered, Shirley sent Stanley back inside to get more milk, which was brought to them, hot and frothy, a few minutes later.

"I don't care what anyone says," Shirley said to him in a loud voice. "The Italians don't know how to make coffee."

At a far table, a young woman looked up and caught Stanley's eye. She was sitting with an older couple and another woman close to her age—her parents and sister, Stanley assumed. He smiled and was relieved when she offered a gentle smile in return. He hoped that she had not understood what Shirley said, but thought it unlikely. When she turned her gaze away, Stanley continued to watch her. Her patrician beauty struck him. Her hair was so dark as to look black, and was long and straight, and caught the glare of the sun that shone down on her exposed table. She had smooth olive skin, deepened, he imagined, by time spent lying at the side of a pool or on a beach. Her face in repose took on a serious, almost sombre aspect, but when she smiled it grew radiant with generous goodwill. It was a lovely face. It made him think of Gloria. She too had had a lovely face. Not like this woman's, though; Gloria's complexion had been sallow, and her cheeks had grown jowly when she was still quite young, but when she'd smiled it had brought about a similar effect. Stanley had loved Gloria's smile and had always done his utmost to keep it on her lips, even when she was ill.

Then Shirley said, "Come on," and gave his arm a shove. "We'll miss Antonio."

Stanley swallowed his coffee, which was bitter but satisfying. He found the waiter inside the café and paid the bill while Shirley waited in the street. On his way out, the young woman caught his eye again.

Somewhat self-consciously, he said, "*Buongiorno.*"

"*Ciao,*" she replied with her sweet smile.

He would have liked to have taken things more slowly, but Antonio now seemed to be in a hurry. Driving back along the cliff road Stanley was struck by the remarkable view it afforded. Capri lay before them like one of the pastels in the Mercato's dining room, crude in its composition but stunning in its effect. And when they reached the other side of the island and stopped the taxi on a bend in the road so they could take a picture of the Faraglioni, Stanley was taken aback by the strength of his emotions at seeing the strange rock formations; the three chalky pinnacles rising out of the turquoise sea filled him with such a sense of desolation.

"God," Shirley said, standing by his side, "I wonder who owns all those yachts." She turned back toward the taxi. "Do any movie stars own any of those yachts, Antonio?"

Antonio, who'd been leaning against the hood of the car, came over next to them. He looked down at the harbour and squinted, as if he could make out one boat from another. "Yes," he said, nodding. "Yes, some of them. And over there," he pointed toward a large, white villa on the opposite cliff. "That is where they go. Very expensive hotel."

Shirley handed him the camera. "Take our picture, will you, Antonio. Make sure you get some of those yachts in it."

At the hotel that morning, Stanley had been up with the sun. He slipped into shorts and a golf shirt and made his way downstairs. No other guests seemed to be awake yet and he found Giuseppe sitting in the dining room with his wife, drinking coffee and eating hard buns and blueberry jam. The landlord jumped to his feet when he saw Stanley and began to set a table for him.

"No," Stanley said, putting up a hand. "I just want some coffee, if that's okay."

"*Si.* Yes, yes. *Uno caffè americano, si.*"

Stanley stood there, not really knowing what to do, while Giuseppe went about preparing his coffee. He smiled at the landlord's wife and said what a lovely morning it was, but she just nodded, not seeming to understand. When Giuseppe brought him the coffee, he nodded a thank you.

"Is it all right if I take it back to my room?" asked Stanley, feeling rather sheepish about his request.

"Yes, of course," said Giuseppe.

In his room again, Stanley was careful not to wake Shirley. He opened the shutter doors and took his coffee out onto the balcony.

Their room overlooked the courtyard. The scent of the lemon trees below mixed with the aroma of his strong coffee and gave Stanley a pleasing sense of calm. There was nothing impressive about the view. It would do little to sell the Mercato to a prospective guest. Directly opposite were the peeling pink stucco walls of terraced apartments, their patios cluttered with hanging laundry and tangled kitchen gardens. To the left, the raised rail lines of the Circumvesuviana, and in the distance beyond, past the stretch of residential sprawl, the faint blue of the Bay of Naples. To the right, the drab modern grey brick of the neighbouring apartment block that fronted onto the Corso Italia. And still, in the quiet of morning, it was a delight. The warmth of the sun, the town just coming to life. It was worth it just for this, Stanley thought: Sant'Agnello at dawn. Gloria would have liked it very much.

—⟋⟋—

Capri Town was horrible, the Piazzetta so overrun that they had to shoulder their way through. When Stanley stopped to get a photograph of the dome of Chiasa Santo Stefano, he was pushed so hard from behind that he nearly dropped the camera, but when he turned and looked into the crowd, no one met his eyes. He wondered how it could be that this town and Anacapri shared the same island. And how too that it was this place that garnered all the attention. It was so dirty, so confused, so unfriendly—no different than Marina Grande below. And from the café terraces that choked the square he felt the stares of patrons as they sat with their espressos, like arbiters in judgment.

Ahead of him, Shirley seemed to lose her way. She was in a hurry to get to the fancy shops on Via Camerelle—Gucci, Ferragamo, the lot, Antonio told them, and cheaper than if they went into Naples. But now she was searching for him, trying to find his face among the throng. Stanley waited and watched her. There was a trace of panic around her eyes. People jostled her as they made their way past. She called his name and a few passersby gave her odd looks. Stanley was less than fifteen feet away, but he might as well have been fifteen miles, for even when he fell into her direct line of sight she could not see him. He remained standing a moment longer, being jostled himself, until her panic began to progress into fear; then he stepped forward and took her by the hand, and when she first looked into his face it was as if she were looking into the face of a stranger.

"Stanley?" she said.

"Yes."

"Oh, Stanley. I thought I lost you."

"No," he said. "I'm right here."

"I think we should go now, Stanley."

"Yes, dear," he said and began to lead her from the square.

They found Antonio back at the taxi rank leaning against the car, smoking a cigarette. He was talking to two other men, who were laughing at something he had just told them. He hadn't seen them approach, and waved a hand at them when Stanley said, "We'd like to go back to Marina Grande now, please."

Then, realizing it was who it was, he put a smile on his face and looked at his watch.

"So soon?" he said.

"Yes," Stanley replied.

"Maybe you like to see Villa Jovis? It is very beautiful."

"No," Stanley said, opening the taxi door for Shirley. "Marina Grande, please."

Antonio shrugged his shoulders and threw his cigarette onto the pavement. He passed a surreptitious comment to the two men as he climbed behind the wheel; again they laughed.

The road to Marina Grande did not bother Stanley as it had before. He knew he could do nothing about the hidden dangers, but now he felt better prepared for them. Shirley put her head on his shoulder. He ran his fingers through her hair and saw that her roots were starting to show their grey again. His kissed her softly on her crown.

"Let's eat at the hotel tonight," he said.

"Yes," said Shirley. "Yes, that sounds nice."

The scooter shop appeared to be closed when they passed it by. The marina itself was quieter, less crowded. Stanley still could not understand its charm.

TO HAVE NOT

FRANKLIN FOWLER CURLED· HIS TOES in the sand and smiled,
then he called to the *cabaña* boy.

"*Hernán, orto maragrita, por favor.*"

"*Si, el Señor Folwer. Immediatamente, señor.*"

Franklin watched as Hernán made his way to the thatch-
roofed bar on the thin strip of grass that separated the Hotel
Vivo's pool from the swath of white-sand beachfront that was
restricted to paying guests. The beach was protected on each
side by thick spans of yellow rope stretched between iron stan-
chions. Hotel guards in dark brown trousers and beige blouses
with flashes on the shoulders patrolled these lengths. Around
their waists they had low-slung white belts with dangling
batons. The guards were not entirely necessary, but they gave
the guests a sense of security, and helped furnish the illusion
that their hotel was of the same class as the bigger resorts
across the bay in Nuevo Vallarta. At those bigger resorts,
better-dressed guards than these policed the beaches for the

beggars and trinket hawkers who descended upon the guests like mosquitos at dusk in the hope of earning a few pesos, or if they were lucky, actual American dollars. Such pedlars and panhandlers did not bother with the Hotel Vivo.

"*Su bebida, el Señor Fowler.*"

"*Gracias tanto, Hernán,*" Franklin said, taking the drink. He licked some salt from the rim, then held the cold glass to his forehead a moment, before setting it into the little hole he had burrowed in the sand beside his beach chair. Then Franklin reached into the canvas bag he had taken to carrying around with him and retrieved two ten-peso notes.

"*Muchos gracias, el Señor Fowler,*" said Hernán and bowed graciously.

Franklin waved his hand: "It's nothing, Hernán. *No es nada.*"

He watched as Hernán made his way once again across the cloying sand toward the bar. When Franklin had first begun spending his afternoons on the beach he'd always gone to the bar himself. He didn't like the thought of Hernán—who, though he was a *cabaña* boy, was several years Franklin's senior—having to struggle across the sand in his heavy-soled shoes to bring him his drink. He thought he was doing the older man a favour. That is until the hotel manager, an ex-pat Brit with a swollen belly and varicose nose, took him aside and explained that the *cabaña* boys depended on tips from the guests to subsidize their otherwise meagre wages.

"I'd no idea," Franklin had said, embarrassed by his miscue. "Have there been complaints?"

"Not complaints exactly," the manager replied. His name was Willy Booth, and Franklin found him rather intimidating.

He leaned in close when he spoke, resting a thick-fingered hand on Franklin's shoulder. It was not so much a posture of confidence as one of implied threat, as if he was offering a warning rather than kindly advice, though never once did the smile pass from his lips, which made it all the worse. "Let's just call it concerns, shall we," Willy said. "These buggers know better than to complain."

From that point on Franklin had allowed himself to be served, or rather paid for the privilege of service. Willy had told him just to throw the boys a few pesos, but Franklin decided on twenty. It was his only real expense apart from his bar tab and club membership, which was what Willy called the nominal fee Franklin had to pay for using the Hotel Vivo's beach, seeing as he was not actually a paying guest of the hotel. Franklin owned a private house on a lagoon farther along the road.

Franklin took a sip of his drink. What a glorious taste, he thought, as the salt mixed with the tart lime and the pungent tequila. He tipped his head back and let the ice slide along his tongue and down his throat before it had a chance to melt. It gave him a quick rush of pain behind his eyes, like when he used to bite into an ice cream as a child. He put his thumb behind his front teeth and pushed hard to relieve the pressure of the cold. It was a trick his mother had taught him. As the ache subsided, he leaned back in his chair and closed his eyes to the sun. This is the life, he told himself, and rubbed a hand across his belly. It was growing fat with leisure; soon it would be big like Willy Booth's.

Willy Booth. Franklin would never have thought it after that first meeting, but without Willy he would be lost. And he half suspected that Willy might be the same without him. Well, if not exactly lost, then at least somewhat more solitary.

It was Willy who forced the issue, inviting Franklin into the bar for a drink that turned into many more and soon became a routine that both looked forward to, though neither would come out and say as much. To see them together, they were an odd couple indeed. There was Willy, his body engorged like a weightlifter gone to pot, his appetite for plea-sure nearly as swollen, and always wearing a smile that only just masked the belligerence residing beneath. Next to him Franklin's weediness was thrown into stark relief: he was spindly arms and spindly legs with only the hint of a paunch pushing out the front of his shirt. And whereas Willy's skin seemed stretched thin over his bulk and barely able to contain him, Franklin looked to have more than he needed—this was most noticeable beneath his chin, where the flesh hung loose like a turkey's wattle, making it appear as if he had once been a much larger man, which wasn't the case.

For his part, Franklin recognized their incongruities, and he was aware that their differences went far deeper than merely the physical. In Willy, Franklin saw a vigour that he craved, and he secretly hoped that some of the big man's excessiveness might rub off on him.

In truth, Franklin began to think of Willy Booth as a godsend, as the conveyance that would deliver him from the deepening rut of his life. He even said as much to him. "Willy," Franklin said one night in the bar, his chair tilted precariously on two legs, his vision blurred by drink, "you are a godsend." Willy looked at him with a pinched expression that forced the blood into the end of his bulbous nose, then refilled their glasses with the Johnny Walker Black he'd commandeered from behind the bar, and said, "Your problem, Fowler, is that you've no romance in your life. *Ningún romance. Ninguna vitalidad. Ninguna aventura.* Know what I mean?"

Franklin knew exactly what Willy meant.

———〰———

When his mother died, Franklin found himself an orphan. He was forty-one years old and, for the first time in his life, alone in the world.

After the funeral, Franklin stood in the kitchen of the house on Montrose Avenue and made himself a cup of coffee. He liked it sweet: three sugars. He took his coffee, and a handful of biscuits from the tray he had brought home from the reception in the basement of St Bart's, and went out into the backyard. He stood by the fence and munched a Chinese rice cracker that to him tasted of nothing, though an elderly friend of his mother told him the crackers were meant to taste like prawns. Franklin had never eaten prawns before.

Below him lay Bickford Park. On the hillside opposite, a number of people had set out towels on the grass and were bathing in the late-May sunshine. A group of older men played bocce at one end of the park, the soft clicking of the balls floating upward on the currents of warm air and mingling with the shouts coming from the baseball diamond below Harbord Street. Franklin watched it all, drinking his coffee and chewing his flavourless biscuits. And while he did, he thought, I have never played baseball, I have never bowled bocce, I have never lain out in the sun.

—⁓—

El Rio Pequeño de Magdalena was not a river at all. Nor was it the enchanting lagoon that the agent in Puerto Vallarta had described. Rather it fell somewhere between a modest inlet and a vast salt marsh.

There were two other properties on the lagoon, both vacant. Each had rather humble plantation-style houses, like Franklin's. But whereas the other two had peeling facades, their columns looking like grey snakes shedding their skin in the sun, the weatherboard walls of La Casa de Mavis—Franklin had named the house after his mother—were painted bright canary yellow. The realtor, an American who ran the Coldwell Banker office in Puerto Vallarta that specialized in holiday homes, had arranged, in a moment of generosity or pity, Franklin wasn't sure, to have the house painted. He also arranged the hiring of a part-time cleaning woman and a part-time gardener, who saw to the upkeep of La Casa de Mavis for the cost of twenty American dollars a week each. Franklin wondered if he might not be able to find even cheaper help, but decided it would be impolite to refuse the man's assistance.

Seen from the far shore of the lagoon, the estate, which was how Franklin liked to refer to it, looked a lovely sight: the bright yellow house standing out like a tropical bloom against the green forest behind, the closely cropped lawn, with newly tilled beds awaiting the planting of multicoloured local flowers, sloping gently toward the water's edge. Close up, though, the lurid paint and shorn grass weren't nearly as convincing; it all looked inconsistent and slapdash. But Franklin didn't mind; it was cheap, it was his, and it didn't overlook Bickford Park.

—⟁—

His mother had managed to pay off the mortgage to the house on Montrose Avenue when Franklin was still in elementary school. She saved the documents that the bank gave her until Victoria Day, then she took her young son out into the back-yard where they filled a steel bucket with dirt. She rolled the documents into a tight tube and planted them in the bucket, so that to Franklin they looked like the beginnings of a little paper tree. Then she took him by the hand and led him to the picnic table, which she decided would be a safe distance. After she sat him down, she smiled sweetly and said, "This will be our own private fireworks."

She went back to the bucket, where she removed a pack of wooden matches from the pocket of her housedress and having lit one, touched its flame to the mortgage papers. Then she stood back and watched them burn.

There was smoke, but very little flame. It was, to say the least, anticlimactic. And Franklin hoped that because of this his mother would relent and take him above Bloor Street to Christie Pits where, after the sun went down, there would be real fireworks. But after the bank papers had smouldered away into a fine grey ash, she took him by the hand again and brought him back into the house. They sat together in the living room and watched *Mannix* with the volume raised to drown out the sound of the Catherine wheels and Roman candles and aerial repeaters that drifted through the night air.

His mother loved *Mannix*. Every week they watched the show, and she'd often told him how Mike Connors was the spitting image of his father. But Franklin had found photographs in his mother's room of her and his father from before he was born, and some from after, of the three of them in hospital when Franklin looked like nothing more than a bundle of blankets. There was no resemblance. Mike Connors had a big chest and thick dark hair and a jaw that was square and strong; his father's hair was patchy and his face mean and pinched. And he ran away before Franklin came home from the hospital.

Franklin could not find the photographs after she died, though in truth he didn't search very carefully for them. He didn't pay much attention to anything when he boxed up her belongings for the Goodwill. He dumped the contents of drawers into cardboard packing crates, then he folded her dresses and laid them on top—so things didn't shift around—before he taped the lids shut. She had only a few books and very little jewellery, so he put those into packing crates, too. It took a day to erase her existence from the house on Montrose Avenue, though it took two months after her death for him to bring himself to do it.

It took far less time to actually sell the place. Franklin accepted the first offer, even though the real estate agent advised him against it. The house on Montrose Avenue had appreciated more than tenfold, and with that money, along with the small stipend from his mother's insurance policy, Franklin had little need to worry, and even less need to work. Which is what he told the principal at St Jude's when he informed him that he would not be returning for the autumn semester. And when the principal asked him what he planned to do, Franklin had replied, "Nothing. Maybe write a book." The thought had never occurred to him before that moment, but he liked it. The only thing he took from the classroom where he had spent every working day for the past eighteen years was a plaster bust of William Shakespeare. When he picked it up, he found that someone had forced chewed wads of paper into the shallow cavities of the Bard's nostrils.

The statue sat now on a table in his study alongside a leather-covered writing tablet and a Mont Blanc fountain pen, and stared blankly out over the sweeping, close-trimmed lawn toward the briny waters of the fraudulent El Rio Pequeño de Magdalena.

—⁓—

"What d'you say to the cockfights?"

Franklin had been looking at his chest. His shirt was pulled open and he was pressing his finger into the skin there, and watching as the pale circle of flesh appeared momentarily, then was swallowed up again by the deep tan surrounding it. He tanned quite well, which surprised him. When he decided on Mexico after having seen a travel documentary on one of the new cable stations, his chief worry was that he would suffer constantly from sunburn. He'd always had a pallid complexion, as had his mother. It seemed such a silly worry now.

"Beg you pardon?" he said to Willy.

"The cockfights. I've got some that want to see the cockfights. Thought you might like to tag along."

"Which ones?

"Which ones, which ones?" parroted Willy, shaking his head. "The proper ones, of course. Outside Punta Minta on the PV road."

Willy Booth, Franklin knew, had a bit of a mean streak in him. It usually showed itself after he'd been drinking. It wasn't so much that he could be cruel as mischievous—or at least mischievous with a touch of malice. He liked to frighten his guests. And the cockfights on the PV road would serve him well if he was in the mood. Unlike the fights that were organized by the franchised resorts in Nuevo Vallarta, the Punta Minta fights were real. The birds wore razors, the pit was bloodstained, and the locals wagered their hard-earned pay. And it wasn't so uncommon for fights to break out among the spectators after they had finished up in the pit.

"What time?" asked Franklin.

"Say half-eight." Willy smiled. "We'll meet up in the bar and have a few drinks before we head out."

Franklin liked Hemingway. And he thought, after he told the people he worked with at St Jude's that he was moving to Mexico to write a book, that he might try something along the lines of *To Have and Have Not* rather than, say, *The Sun Also Rises* or *The Old Man and the Sea*, each of which he'd had to teach ad nauseam to his bored pupils. It was the adventure of the former that drew him: the idea of Harry Morgan sitting in the Perla eating black bean soup and looking out the new window that replaced the one that had been shot out, all the while waiting to meet the smugglers he'd been forced by necessity to work with. He liked to imagine himself as Harry, a good man driven to desperate measures. And that was how he saw himself as he sat at his table in La Bodequita, the Hotel Vivo's little bar. He was drinking Dos Equis—he liked its black bottle—while Willy waited in the lobby to collect the guests who wanted to go to the cockfights.

Unlike the Hotel Vivo's beach, La Bodequita was open to locals. It managed to avoid any unpleasantness by imposing a two-drink minimum for non-guests and selling its liquor at exorbitant prices. This, along with the other customary bar rules, was enforced by the same guards who looked after the beach, though in La Bodequita they exchanged their warden uniforms for dark trousers and white golf shirts with the hotel's logo stitched over the breast. Still, Franklin liked to imagine that among the bar's patrons there might be smugglers and gangsters and women of ill repute. And sipping his beer he glanced about with a wary eye, trying to spot the dangerous characters.

"Mr Sing show up yet?"

It was Willy; he'd come in from the lobby and stood behind Franklin's chair. He had a grin on his face, and by the angle of it, it was clear that he already had a few drinks in him.

"Still waiting," said Franklin.

"Any *gallegos* I should be worried about?" Willy asked as he motioned for Miguel at the bar to bring him a whisky.

"I think you're all right for tonight," replied Franklin, pushing out a chair for him.

"Good," said Willy, and he sat down. "The last thing I need is to have my windows shot out again."

This banter had become their private joke. Six months earlier, and two months after he had moved into La Casa de Mavis, Franklin, after a long night in the bar, had told Willy about his bookish ideas and the little fantasy game he played with himself in La Bodequita. It was, he had realized, probably a mistake. But the next morning, Willy drove into Puerto Vallarta and found a copy of *To Have and Have Not* and read it the same afternoon. He hadn't thought much of the book, but agreed with Franklin that there was something appealing about Harry Morgan. "The way he gives it to that tourist cow in Freddy's," he said the next time they were drinking, "I liked that bit."

At first Franklin was uncomfortable about Willy's having read the book; it almost felt to Franklin as if something had been taken away from him. And he thought that Willy'd done it just so he could poke fun. But then Franklin found that he didn't mind the gag so much, especially when he noted the few occasions when their little exchange caught the attention of those sitting at the nearer tables; he enjoyed the thought that it might lend him a slightly mysterious quality.

"Well," said Willy, using his forefinger to stir the ice in his glass before taking a drink, "I think we might make a good showing tonight."

Franklin knew that this meant one of two things: either Willy had his eye on one of the female guests, or, failing that, he had decided to amuse himself at the expense of his clientele. Either way, it made Franklin a touch uneasy.

Willy swallowed the rest of his whisky and offered Franklin a crooked smile: "It's time, Fowler. *Tengamos una aventura.*"

"Sorry?"

"For God's sake, man," Willy said, his voice booming through the bar. "An adventure."

He stood up and clapped his hands on Franklin's shoulders. "Let's see if we can't shake your life up a little."

—ᴍᴠ—

Franklin recognized early on that his needs were more a reflec-
tion of his mother's neediness than of his own necessity. He
was her life, or rather his life was hers. It had been conferred
by his father's betrayal, as if it were surety. And Mavis Fowler
was determined that another would not get away from her.
Franklin understood this—understood that constant compan-
ionship made up the terms of the agreement. At times he felt
as if the house on Montrose Avenue were a prison, that the
fence in the backyard was a high wall topped with razor wire
and that the sounds coming from Bickford Park were the
sounds of freedom. At other times he was plagued with a guilt
that was not his own. For Franklin the might of guilt proved
more powerful than hunger for liberty. And because it was so,
he instigated very little in his life, waiting instead for direction from her. Until he was forty-one years old, he slept every
night in the bedroom directly across the hallway from hers, his
door open so he would hear if she called. Now, at La Casa de
Mavis, he kept a picture of her on his bedside table.

Willy found it there on the one occasion that Franklin
invited him round to see the estate.

"Who's this, then?" he said, picking it up and studying it
closely. "Pining after an old flame, are you, Fowler?"

"No," Franklin said, taking the picture from him and carefully replacing it on the side table. "My mother."

Willy stared at the photograph as if the notion was foreign
to him, as if he was not quite certain what a mother was. Then
he laughed.

"She's a looker, your mum," he said. "Bet she'd of liked me."

"No," Franklin replied. "I think it's a safe bet that she wouldn't have."

—⁓—

The first time Franklin went to the cockfights on the PV road outside Punta Minta it had been Independence Day. The flat, hard-packed earth surrounding the low-slung wooden building had been turned into something of a fairground, with a Ferris wheel and swing rides and a brief midway crowded with carnival games and vendors selling *carne asada* and *tamales* and *sopaipillas*. In the small cramped arena the air was festive and families gathered to watch the fights; out back, children played in the dead piles.

But it was a different place during the night fights. No carnival, no families, no frivolity; at night it smelled of sweat and mescal and tobacco.

On the drive out, Franklin sat in the front passenger seat of the hotel van feeling queasy. He remained quiet as Willy, driving as well half-drunk as he did fully sober, chattered on to his guests in the back. Only three of the original six had decided to go through with the excursion. The others had timidly bowed out at the last moment. It hardly seemed worth it to Franklin, but Willy had his mind set. He'd charged each of the guests ten dollars American, though it only cost twelve pesos to get into the fights. The three *gamers*, as Willy called them, were a young married couple from Buffalo and a middle-aged woman from Bangor, Maine, whose girlfriend had begged off and stayed behind at the hotel. This was the one, Franklin decided, that Willy had his eye on.

"I was just thinking," said the young husband, who worked in a bakery but fancied himself something of a photographer. "I'm probably gonna need to use a flash in there."

"Well now, Mr Pollack," Willy said, looking at the man in the rear-view mirror, "I wouldn't suggest it."

"That gonna be a problem?" the young baker asked. Franklin didn't like his smug tone.

"No, not at all," replied Willy, casting a sideways glance at Franklin and giving him a wink. "Not if you don't mind some no-good *gallego* cutting the strap and making off with your lovely Minolta."

"Is that likely to happen?" asked the woman from Bangor. "I mean, is this a dangerous place you're taking us to, Mr Booth?"

"Well, Ms Leggett . . . Christina—d'you mind if I call you Christina? It's a lovely name, that. Reminds me of Christmas."

Franklin watched as Willy managed to flirt with the woman sitting directly behind him, impressed at how easily he did so without once taking his eyes from the road, and without giving in to the urge to witness her reaction.

"What you must understand, Christina," he went on, "is that where I'm taking you is the real Mexico. Not the make-believe, play-land Mexico that the Jar Tar Village and Club Marival over in Nuevo Vallarta subject their guests to, but the real salt-of-the-earth Mexico. And I think it best we don't draw too much attention to ourselves."

"Maybe he's right, Pat," said the young baker's doughy young wife, sounding nervous. "You should probably just leave the flash in the van."

From their seats on the rickety wooden bleachers they had a clear view of the pit. The air in the arena was thick with the smell of damp hay, with the faint underlying scent of urine. The judges had weighed the birds and the odds were set. The cockfighters readied their *gallos*. The one nearest to where they were sitting sprayed a mouthful of beer into his bird's face, while the other took his rooster's beak between his lips and blew hard so that his cheeks puffed out like Dizzy Gillespie's. Then the two men came together in the centre of the pit, their birds held out at arm's length. On the judge's signal, they tossed the birds at one another.

Franklin could feel Christina Leggett flinch beside him. The pit below erupted in a cloud of dust and feathers, and there came mild sounds of encouragement from the crowd that, until that point, had seemed all but ignorant of the goings-on in the small wooden enclosure. As the birds pecked and chased one another in circles, interest grew audibly, punctuated by shrill whistles from someone on the bleacher off to the side.

"This isn't so bad," said the baker, who sat to Franklin's left, eyeing it all through his camera lens.

"They haven't started yet," Franklin said.

"What do you mean?" the young man replied, looking accusingly at him.

Franklin hoped that Willy would get back soon. He'd left them after they'd found their seats, saying he was off to lay a bet. And when he disappeared beneath the bleachers, rather than going to one of the judges at ringside, Franklin reasoned that he must have decided to place his wager with a private bookie. It was often done at the night fights; the bookies

tended to give better odds than did the judges. Then he saw
Willy behind the stands on the far side of the arena passing
money to two young men, one in dirty jeans and a checked
shirt, the other dressed similarly but wearing a straw cowboy
hat. Franklin just wanted him to hurry up and finish with it
already. He didn't relish the idea of having to play the host,
especially to Mr Pollack, whom he found terribly unpleasant.

"They're just warming up," Franklin said, scanning the
crowd, having lost sight of Willy again. "It's like a trial run.
They do it to get the birds agitated."

"That seems rather cruel," said Christina Leggett, leaning
in slightly against Franklin's shoulder.

"It is," he said. "But it gets worse."

Franklin liked very much that she was sitting beside him,
he liked that their shoulders were touching, but he couldn't
help wonder what it was that made her want to be there. If
the mock fight disturbed her, what would she think once
the blades were unwrapped? Would she shudder at the sight?
Clutch his arm? Or would she be fascinated, thrilled even,
by the violence of it all? Franklin could accept it if she was,
because he understood morbid curiosity, fathomed that
impulse that drove people to regard the unseemly. It was
there in the funeral home when he'd stood over Mavis's
open coffin, wondering what would happen if he gave in to
the urge to press his fingers into her waxy face and push her
lips into a smile and then a frown and a crooked smirk.
Someone, he couldn't remember who, had led him back to
a chair, thinking that he was overcome, when really all he
was doing was trying to decide if any of the expressions
would hold, or whether there was enough resilience left in

her flesh to draw her lips again into the eternal grimace she always wore.

"I trust Fowler's been keeping you all entertained," said Willy, who was making his way up the steps of the bleacher. He was carrying five quart bottles of beer, the necks of them wedged between his fat fingers. He shuffled his way along their row and plunked himself down on the other side of Ms Leggett. "When in Rome," he said as he passed the bottles down the line.

"My God," said Ms Leggett. "This tastes horrible."

"Indeed it does, Christina," said Willy. "But I promised you honest-to-goodness Mexico, and that's what you shall have." Then he looked along the row past Franklin and said, "Isn't that right, Master Pollack?"

The young baker took a healthy swig from the bottle and swallowed, trying to hide his distaste, as if taking the drink had been a challenge. His wife held her bottle out in front of her as though it was something toxic.

"Go on, love," Willy said to her. "Be a trooper. It'll put hair on your chest, that." Then quietly to himself: "Or take it off."

Franklin drank his own without complaint. It was bitter, with a slightly chemical tang, but it was cold and quenched the thirst he had built up in Willy's absence.

"Which did you take?" he asked, leaning forward to see around Ms Leggett.

"What's that?" said Willy.

"Your bet?" said Franklin and pointed toward the pit. "The bantam or the Cornish?"

"Oh, that," smiled Willy. "I decided to give it a miss. Both a little on the small side for my liking."

The first fight was quick and bloody. When the birds were brought together again in the centre of the pit, blades tied to their spurs, it was the bantam that lunged first, using its diminutive size to get in low on the Cornish and sink a razor into its breast. The judge held up a hand to allow time for the Cornish to be revived. The owner picked up his bird and took its beak into his mouth, but unlike before he did not blow; rather he sucked, then spat a mouthful of blood into the dirt.

"Punctured lung," Willy said. "Should of bet the wee one."

Almost as soon as the fight was restarted it was over. The bantam rose up in a flap and came down again on the other's back, its blades slicing through the Cornish's neck, sending a thin spurt of blood out over the dirt floor, its intensity receding with each pulse. As the shouts rang out from the crowd, the bantam began to peck at the eyes of the dying bird.

While they remained for two more fights, it was clear to Franklin that the others' hearts were no longer in it. Mrs Pollack had grown very quiet; so too had her husband, though he continued to snap photographs, even after she told him that he'd taken more than enough. Beside Franklin, Christina Leggett had physically stiffened; she sat with a very straight back and she'd wrapped her arms tightly across her chest. He wondered if maybe he shouldn't touch her somehow, just to let her know that it was all right, that what she'd seen was just something ugly and nothing more, like his mother in her casket—just a bit of unpleasantness. But Franklin was not good at offering comfort, just as he was not good at receiving it. The handshakes, the embraces, the sorry palms against his cheek were, for him, the most uncomfortable aspect of his mother's funeral. Neither was he able to offer words of relief to the few old women who had come to mourn. It was not that he lacked compassion, simply the skill to act upon it.

Willy saw nothing unpleasant. He was enjoying himself immensely. He cheered as loud as the locals and placed bets on both the other fights. He lost each time, but did not seem bothered. Nor did he seem all that bothered when Franklin suggested they leave. He knew enough to know that his guests had had their fill. They'd seen their bit of native culture and were predictably put off by it. And Franklin had to admit that he'd been put off by it as well. All told, it had been a gruesome affair that left him feeling sick in his guts, which he did well to hide. Though he didn't but wonder how Harry Morgan would have felt, or Hemingway himself for that matter—likely they wouldn't have been bothered; likely they would have seen it as Willy had: an exciting sport and a worthy pastime.

Outside the arena the air was much cooler and sweet scented. And if not for the crowding of cars and pickup trucks and the muffled din drifting out of the building to their backs, it would have seemed another world. As they picked their way through the parking lot there came the faint sound of *ranchera* music being played on a car radio. Willy began to hum along to it, and when Franklin heard the voices, he thought it was Willy singing.

"*Denos su dinero.*"

Franklin had taken a few more steps before he realized that the others had stopped walking. When he turned around he didn't see the two men, not until the one said, "*Sobre aquí, imbécil,*" and stepped toward him with the knife. He moved it slowly back and forth so that the moonlight caught its edge. All Franklin could think was, It doesn't even look real.

"*Denos su dinero,*" the one with the knife said again.

The other man, who was slightly taller, and wore his straw cowboy hat pushed back off his forehead, motioned toward the young baker and said, "*Y la cámara.*"

Franklin looked at Willy; he had his hands raised high over his head.

"I think," he said, "we should do as they say."

When he was fourteen years old, three kids in the grade above Franklin had caught him in the school washroom. While two of the boys held him down, pinning his shoulders against the cold parquet floor, the third leaned over him and dribbled spit onto his face. They laughed as the string of gob fell onto the bridge of his nose, then snailed its way along his cheek until it pooled in the recess of his ear. Afterward, the boys emptied the books from his bag and stuffed them into a toilet; they made Franklin flush the toilet before they left him.

In the wake of this assault, Franklin was left feeling not so much frightened as completely hollow. It was as if the fear that had first entered him had somehow eaten its way out of his body, leaving behind only his shell. He left his books in the toilet bowl, swollen and ruined, and ran the four blocks from the school to the house on Montrose Avenue. He did not tell Mavis what had happened, but asked to be fed. For the rest of the afternoon he ate everything that she put before him, trying to fill the emptiness he'd been left with. He ate so much that he was sick; and then after he was sick, he ate more.

Sitting in La Bodequita he felt that same emptiness again. But it wasn't the two men who made him feel this way; rather, it was Willy. Willy, who sat across the table and filled their glasses again with ice that he'd taken from the bucket with his hands; Willy, who poured whisky over the ice so that it cracked loudly as it began to melt; Willy, who picked up his own tumbler and sat back in his chair looking satisfied with himself.

"But what I want to know," Franklin said, "is why?"

"Oh, come on, Fowler. It was just a bit of fun."

Franklin shook his head. "They were really scared."

"Nonsense," Willy said, taking a drink. "I gave them a wonderful story to take home and tell their friends."

"I don't think Christina thought it was wonderful," said Franklin, recalling the blankness of the expression on her face and the way her hands shook as she emptied her pockets for them.

"Ah, yes." Willy smiled. "Darling Christina."

Franklin didn't like the way he said her name, how he pursed his lips afterward and ran his tongue across his teeth, as if he tasted the remnants of her.

"I thought you were in there, Fowler."

"What do you mean?" said Franklin.

"Our little Ms Leggett; our dear Christina," Willy said, his smile becoming a leer. "I thought you were made in the shade, in like Flynn. What with the way she was rubbing up against you at the fights. And then the way she looked to you when Juan and Simón did their piece."

"I've no idea what you're talking about," Franklin said. He picked up his glass and took a long sip—the empty feeling, he thought he might be able to drink it away.

"Now I'll admit," Willy went on, "at first I considered her for myself. But she was a little too matronly for my tastes, a little too Mother Hubbard. Know what I mean? A bit too dowager. I like mine a touch more frisky. Still, she was good for you, I thought. Tell you something else: I was half hoping that you were going to put on a show for her. You know, have it out with Juan right there in the car park. He'd have been up for it, would of given you a good little tussle. Nothing too rough, of course. He's a good lad, that one. Now Simón. He would of dropped the bloody knife and legged it. He's useless, he is. Still, either one would of done it for you, would of delivered the lovely Christina wrapped up in a bow."

Looking at him, Franklin noticed for the first time how truly ugly Willy Booth actually was: his big belly stretching out his shirt, his arms fat and smooth, his hair cut short to distract from his growing baldness, his limpid eyes lost in a face that was a crimson map of alcoholic rosacea. And seeing all this, Franklin felt sorry for him.

"I don't think we should be talking about Ms Leggett this way," he said.

Willy just shook his head. "*Ninguna aventura. Ningún romance*," he said. "You remember me saying that?"

"Yes," Franklin said, knowing that Willy was right. There had been a moment there in the car park, though to call it an opportunity would be crude. It was a chance to act; Franklin recognized it when Simón looked to Willy, as if for direction, before he and Juan fled into the night. What would Christina have thought if he'd stepped forward in the instant, taken things in hand? He would never know. "It was just a cruel trick, Willy."

"Oh, for Chrissakes, Fowler. They got exactly what they wanted," said Willy, sounding indignant now. "Besides, that bloody Pollack is a little prick. He deserved to have the shit scared out of him. I've a mind to let Simón keep his pissy little camera."

Willy got quiet after that, but as he sat there the redness in his face deepened, and watching him, Franklin got the impression that he was very much like a shaken bottle of soda, the pressure building from within. But then Willy laughed. He leaned forward in his chair and set his glass on the table, and was laughing still as he picked up the bottle and poured himself more whisky.

"'Travel is a fool's paradise,'" he said through his happy grin. "You ever hear that saying, Fowler? 'Travel is a fool's paradise.'"

"Yes," Franklin said. "It's Emerson."

"If you say so," said Willy. "You're the one who knows the books. I just think it's funny. Maybe I'll use it as my motto. Stick it up in the office, right over my desk. I'll look up at it every time I have to deal with the likes of that Pollack."

"'We owe to our first journeys the discovery that place is nothing.'"

"What's that then?" asked Willy.

"It's the rest of the quote," said Franklin.

"Yeah?" said Willy. "I don't know if I like that part much. Bit wordy, that."

Franklin just shrugged.

"You going to stay for one more?" asked Willy, holding up the bottle.

Franklin closed his eyes a moment and thought of La Casa de Mavis, and of his mother's photograph waiting for him on the night table beside his bed, and of the empty journal and the Mont Blanc fountain pen and the statue of Shakespeare looking out toward the salt marsh in the dark. And of Christina Leggett in her room upstairs, a chair wedged under her door handle, the shutters to her balcony locked, her covers pulled up tight under her chin, awake and frightened— or maybe she was asleep and dreaming something nice.

He pushed his glass across the table. "Sure, Willy," he said. "Why not."

MAXIM'S TROUT

THE FAMILIAR PAIN FLARES in his belly: a charcoal briquette beneath his ribcage, waiting for the lighter fluid of his daily life to feed it with flame. To imagine his ailment in terms of a barbecue is the only way Bull Maxim can deal with the discomfort. It makes the whole thing somehow more manageable: he knows his way around a barbecue. He unscrews the top from the economy-size bottle of Maalox and takes a long swallow, envisioning the cloudy fluid racing down into the fat-boy Hibachi and smothering the cinders. It doesn't work, of course. The antacid lost its curative value some months back. Bull drinks it now simply for the taste. The cool, chalky flavour soothes him. More often now, Bull finds that when he awakes in the night with a thirst it isn't Marlene's homemade iced tea or Darryl's diet cola he reaches for, but the Maalox. He likes how it leaves a gluey film on his tongue, even if it does sour his breath. Then again, Marlene kisses him so infrequently now that it doesn't seem to matter.

Bull had been hopeful that Dr Carey could help him, even accepted his advice and went to a city hospital. He swallowed barium, lay still like an expectant mother for an ultrasound, closed his eyes for the proctologist, but there was nothing. His gallbladder was fine, as were his liver, pancreas and appendix. There were no tumours on his colon, no tears in his oesophagus, no ulcers in his stomach. "A nervous tummy, is all," Dr Carey said in the end. His only suggestion was to stay away from Marlene's chili. "Just relax and enjoy life, Bull."

Just relax and enjoy life, Bull thinks, as he quietly pulls a chair out from the kitchen table. He can't even relax and enjoy sleep. The last time he made it all the way through to morning is a distant memory. If it isn't Marlene's indifference playing on his mind, it's Darlene's bitterness. His daughter hates him, more now than ever. And there's Darryl and his flower picking. Bull takes another swallow of Maalox and looks down at himself. His big barrel of a chest and wide round belly hide his briefs from view so that his slightly bowed, newel-post legs appear to sprout from either side of his navel. His hands are meaty and his arms like shanks. His mother named him Rudolph after Valentino, but everyone else just calls him Bull. When he was in high school so many years ago, before football players dressed like spacemen, the people used to chant "*Toro, toro*" when he stepped onto the field. Four years all-county MVP and Rudolph was gone forever. Even when Marlene agreed to take him at the altar, it was Bull.

With antacid in hand, Bull gets up from the table and creeps out of the kitchen. On the front porch he takes a deep breath. The air is still warm from the day and, though he knows it isn't possible, Bull thinks he can smell Morrow. Just knowing that he is out there in the woods with his army of scraggly haired minions seems enough to effect his odour. What they are doing he doesn't want to imagine. There is talk that they are tunnelling, but that makes no sense to Bull. Tunnellers protest logging and this has nothing to do with trees.

A breeze picks up and Bull feels a slight chill. He considers going back inside for his robe; it wouldn't do to have the mayor seen wandering about in the middle of the night in his underpants. But the thought of perhaps waking Marlene stops him. Besides, the mayor in his skivvies wouldn't be much of an oddity. Not any more.

The pain in his belly flares again.

"Goddamn fish," Bull mutters.

Billy Finnegan brought it to him. Dropped it in the dirt at his feet. Bull had been pulling weeds from between his toma- toes and had only just stood to ease the ache in his lower back. When the kids were younger they used to help him with the garden. Marlene helped then, too. Now Bull tended the vegetable patch on his own. He was wiping sweat from the back of his thick neck when Finnegan appeared.

"What the hell is that?" Bull asked.

"It's a fish," Finnegan said.

"I can see that, Billy. What I want to know is why the hell you're throwing it in my garden?"

"I pulled it out of the old quarry."

Billy Finnegan was a poacher. A not very good one, as far as Bull was concerned. During his time as a game warden, before he became mayor, Bull had had many dealings with Finnegan. He was a sloppy trapper and moved through the bush like a bulldozer. It took very little effort for Bull to track him. And more often than not, Bull would find a thankful Billy waiting for him, his snare wire in a loop on his belt, his illegal game in a bag by his feet, himself lost in the woods. Billy Finnegan's sense of direction was atrocious.

"How many times I told you, Billy," Bull said, stepping carefully between the rows, "to stay away from that place? Christ, the kids don't even go up there drinking any more."

Finnegan shrugged and bent down for the fish. Two beanstalks succumbed to his heavy boots as he followed Bull.

"You know how many overgrown shafts there are out there?" Bull said, hiding his anger. "The duck hunters don't even bother with it." Bull himself wouldn't venture out to the old marble quarry. The landscape was speckled with flues that had been dug in the last few years before the quarry shut down; they'd swallowed up enough good bird dogs to convince even the most fanatical hunters that the river was the place to shoot.

Bull offered Finnegan a seat, and watched as the weedy man misjudged the depth and landed with a thump that jarred the fish loose from his grasp. Finnegan left the fish in the grass and rubbed his buttocks.

"So, what can I do for you, Billy," Bull asked, taking a seat beside him.

"It's this thing," Finnegan said, pushing the fish toward Bull with the toe of his boot. "What do you make of it?"

"A trout," Bull said, uninterested.

"Yeah," Finnegan said, leaning forward. "But what kind? I ain't never seen anything like it."

Bull took a closer look. There was no question that it was a trout. The sleek but strong body with its thick tail, the cut of the dorsal and caudal fins said as much. But the colours, Bull thought, weren't right. For a moment he considered it might be a brook, but there were no speckles or spots, and the olive green of its back was far too dark. Then there was the silver colouring on the leading edge of its pectoral fins. It was no brook trout.

"You say you caught it at the quarry?" Bull said.

"Yessir."

"How did it fight?"

"Didn't fight at all. Thing was dead by the time I pulled it in."

Sitting now on the porch steps, Bull can hear Darlene climbing down the lattice. The thin wood strains under her weight and the vines caught up in her clothes snap free from their hold. It's a wonder there is any ivy left, she's made the descent so often. His daughter is escaping later tonight than usual, owing to Bull's lingering in front of the television—an old black-and-white film he paid little attention to. He'd done so hoping Darlene might fall asleep in her bed and miss her late-night rendezvous. No such luck. His dawdling would succeed in nothing more than strengthening her ire. There seems little Bull can do to staunch his daughter's ill will. She loathed him even before the fish, but it was an expected malignity: parent and teenage child. Now her mordancy is feral. When she looks at him now there is not only contempt in her eyes, but abhorrence.

He watches her as she slips around the side of the house. Her long hair is tied in knots at the sides and top of her head. He can see the weak gleam of the stud she's pushed through the bottom of her lip. The skin must be still swollen and tender, he figures, seeing the awkward way she keeps her mouth open. She's cut the legs off her favourite pair of jeans and wears them over thick black leotards that disappear into an old pair of Darryl's workboots. An old cardigan of Marlene's is thrown overtop a newly torn black T-shirt. She must be very warm, Bull thinks.

At the street she stops and turns back to look at him. Bull waits for her to say something, another stinging insult that has become usual in the past few weeks. He misses the old taunts born of adolescent angst: harsh but never hurtful. The ones that made him feel like a father. Now she treats him like the enemy, and her scorn cuts deeply.

Bull waves. Darlene walks away without responding.

"Fantastic!" Morrow said, leaning close to the fish. "No, more than fantastic. Maybe a miracle, at least scientifically speaking. It's just so beautiful," he cooed, stroking the stiff scales.

Bull hadn't wanted to come, but after exhausting his own guidebooks and those of the Marbleton library he didn't know where else to turn. Morrow was definitely the man. He called himself an aquatic biologist. Bull had no idea what that meant. Nor did Morrow fit with Bull's notion of a scientist: white lab coat, close-cut hard-parted hair, thick black-framed glasses—like the men from detergent commercials on the television, the ones who placed large checkmarks on their

clipboards. As far as Bull was concerned, Morrow looked like
a bum, a vagrant off the street. His was gangly and wore a
scrubby beard. His hair sprouted like a bush from his scalp,
and his clothes looked stiff from lack of washing. Then there
was his voice, which croaked and wavered like a pubescent
teenager's. But for Bull, the most unnerving thing about the
man was his odour. He smelled like a dead carp lying out in
the sun. Granted, Morrow concentrated his efforts on fish,
their physiology, cytology, histology and propagation—Bull
had many times helped Morrow and his students count pick-
erel and set lamprey traps—but the tang seemed not to reside
on his skin so much as emanate from within.

Bull wasn't too keen on visiting the university either. First
off there was the drive. Not that an hour on the road was
overly long, but his old Dodge Ram wasn't in the greatest of
shape. The transmission had been ready to give out for a few
months already. So to be sure he could make it to the university and back, Bull drove at half the speed limit, which added
another hour to the trip and attracted a wealth of horn blasts
and raised fingers.

Neither was it a mean feat trying to find Morrow's office. First
off, the university was not what he'd expected. Bull had imagined it like a high school, only bigger. He'd figured on walking
into a reception office and having a secretary direct him down a
hallway or two to his destination. Instead, he discovered what at
first glance appeared to be a small city. Buildings, some low to
the ground, others climbing several storeys into the air, were
laid out over countless acres. And there was nothing in the way
of signage that identified any of them. After finding a parking
spot in one of the farthest lots, Bull made his way along a cinder

path that led finally to a wide concrete quadrangle. It was crowded with students, some passing from one building to the next, but most just reclining on benches, enjoying the late-summer sun. The first student Bull asked, a young man with a string of beads in his hair, looked at him and said, "Huh?" When Bull asked again, the man closed his eyes and shook his head. "Sorry, dude," he said. "Don't know your guy."

This happened several more times. It appeared to Bull that Morrow hadn't made much of an impression at the university, or maybe it was just so large that it was impossible to expect him to be readily known. At last someone offered assistance. A girl who looked to Bull as if she had something very bitter tasting in her mouth pointed to a Lego-like building across the river. "It's the Science Complex you want," she said. "Just take the bridge over." Bull thanked her and she smirked, or so it seemed to him.

A security guard laughed when Bull asked where he might find Dr Morrow's office. But when Bull did not respond, he directed him to a stairwell. "Even when you think you can't go any farther," the security guard said, "just keep on going." And he wasn't lying. More than once Bull thought he'd come to the end of the line, the subterranean corridor halting in a tangle of water pipes, heating vents and loose insulation, only to find that the passage continued. When it did finally termi-nate, Bull did not have to read the thin metal tag on the steel fireproof door to know that he'd at last found Dr Morrow. The smell had told him as much.

"Fantastic!" Morrow cried again, leaving the fish on his desk and moving to a cluttered bookshelf. "Help yourself to coffee," he said to Bull.

The coffee machine, the kind Joe DiMaggio used to peddle, was on a small table in the corner of the room. Bull had to step around several piles of books and a crumpled pair of hip waders. Morrow's office was beyond messy. The wastebasket was overflowing and candy wrappers and pop cans littered most every surface. There were two recycling containers beside the small table, but both were empty. And the coffee looked as if it had been brewed days ago. Bull laid his hand on the side of the pot. It was cold.

"Yes," Morrow called out from behind. "Yes, here it is." He motioned Bull back to his desk. "Sit, sit, sit."

Bull removed a stack of typewritten pages from a chair and sat down. Morrow spilled forth like an adolescent caffeine addict. Not only did Bull have trouble distinguishing words, but sentences too were lost to him. The snippets he did pick out made no sense to him. "Industrial Revolution . . . cargo liners . . . pleasure craft." "Blasting" caught his ear only because of his constituency's former industry. Then Morrow stopped. It took Bull a moment to realize he'd gone silent: the professor's gibber still echoed in his ear.

"Mr Mayor," Morrow said—he always referred to Bull by title. "Have you ever heard of the myotonic goat?"

Bull looked at him stupidly. "What does this have to do with a goat?"

"The myotonic goat," Morrow went on, undeterred, "is a scientific, or rather genetic anomaly. It's called by some, ranchers mostly who like their names a little more colourful, the Tennessee Stiff-Leg. Here, look at this."

Morrow pushed an open textbook across the desk, knocking a half-eaten Snickers to the floor. Bull looked at the

picture. A billy goat with straight horns and a beard, its mark-
ings fairly conventional black and white patches.

"Seems pretty regular to me," Bull said.

"Yes," Morrow said, his voice cracking with excitement.
"But walk up behind this animal and clap your hands, Mr
Mayor, and you will find it is anything but regular. In
moments of alarm the body stiffens, the muscles actually seize,
become as rigid as this desk, and the goat literally falls over in
a faint. It is quite, quite fascinating. And if I am not mistaken
sir," Morrow said, a smile cracking his face as he laid his hand
on the dead fish, "we are looking at the same here."

The smart thing would have been to dig a hole in the garden
and drop the bloody thing in, Bull thinks. Fish make good
fertilizer. His mother used to pay the old man across the street
to supply her with perch and sunfish. She'd lay them out in
the sun for a couple of days, then till them into the soil around
her peas and tomatoes and string beans. She never used them
around the potatoes or carrots, though, believing the stink
would get into the root vegetables. That's what I should have
done, Bull tells himself. Instead, he'd wrapped it in
Cellophane and newspaper and stuck it in the deep-freeze,
under bags of rhubarb so Marlene wouldn't find it.

The Jericho trout, Morrow had called the fish. He called it
that after Bull screwed up his face at *Salvelinus rigeo*. He'd
never been good with Latin, already a dead language when he
failed it back in high school. Morrow read the description
aloud from a mouldy leather-bound book. It had sounded like
the same fish, right down to the silver on the pectoral fins. But

the trout Morrow spoke of hadn't been seen since the 1912
gaming expedition on which Sir Holyfield Lewis, an English
gentleman, had made the last recorded sighting. That particular fish became the centrepiece of a lavish banquet at which
the unfortunate Lewis perished, after a fine rib bone became
lodged in his throat, inducing a choking fit that culminated in
a massive coronary. Morrow found the last point very humor-
ous, and his laughter, a combination of snorts and squeals,
unsettled Bull.

He shouldn't have left the damn fish with Morrow
either. A second chance gone. He'd picked it up after their
meeting, but Morrow had grabbed his arm, a tight wiry grip.
"No, please, Mr Mayor. Please." Bull had been happy just to
be rid of the thing. At least that's what he'd thought. Now
Morrow and his flakes are creeping around the woods. And
Darlene is with them. The porch steps are growing cold
beneath his buttocks.

"You'll get piles sitting there like that, Pop."

Darryl's voice spooks him. Bull did not hear his son slip out
the front door, and when he turns to look at him he feels a
great sadness. Darryl is a large boy, more puffy than fat. He has
Bull's height but Marlene's delicate features, and the thin
equine nose and small parchment ears leave him looking
inconsistent. He rarely smiles.

"What are you doing up so late?" Bull asks.

"Darlene woke me," Darryl replies and moves to lean
against the railing.

He is wearing a matching pair of pyjamas with tiny cars
racing across the fabric. He has always worn pyjamas and it
bothers Bull. It was fine when he was younger, though Bull

himself stopped dressing for bed when he was still in grade school. But Darryl is nineteen now; he should be sleeping in his underpants like everyone else.

Like everyone else. Bull knows that is the last thing Darryl will be. And not just because he is big and uncoordinated; or because he doesn't like sports, or fishing or hunting. And not because he collects wildflowers and doesn't like girls. Bull knows this about his son: that he doesn't like girls. That he prefers boys. There is no hiding his effeminacy, which in itself doesn't ensure what his mother called *the delicacy*, though Bull has known of his persuasion since Darryl was quite young. There are things that cannot be hidden, that should not be hidden, Bull thinks. But these are not the things that keep Darryl from being like others. It is something else, the something that saddens Bull every time he looks at him: absence of hope.

Darryl is, in the truest sense of the word, a hopeless person. And this despair stains him like a bruise. His deficiencies, as Marlene calls them, only serve to darken the blemish. Bull wishes he could pick Darryl up, all 265 pounds of him, and drop him down some place where he could be happy. Some place that is not Marbleton, where he doesn't have to live in his father's shadow, with his mother's disappointment or under the unkind gaze of his neighbours. But Bull has never said this to his son.

"How's your stomach, Pop?" Darryl asks, concern in his voice.

Bull hoists the bottle of Maalox and holds it as if on display. "Same as ever," he says.

Darryl nods his head and for a moment appears lost in thought.

"You know," he says, finally, "we should really do something about that."

———✺———

Marlene was angry. Bull could tell by the way her eyebrows were pinched together and her lips drawn into a tight little line. He expected that at any moment she was going to dig the air freshener from beneath the sink and spray it directly into Dr Morrow's face. Not that he would blame her. Morrow's fishy stink had already permeated the entire room, and Bull was becoming concerned that it might seep into the uphol-stery of the couch upon which the man sat, with his feet tucked up underneath him no less.

"I'm thinking, Mr Mayor," Morrow said, rubbing his hands disconcertingly across his breasts, "that the best course of action would be to cordon the entire quarry. A police barri-cade, if you will."

"We don't have any police in Marbleton," Bull said.

"None?"

Bull shook his head.

"Then what do you propose we do, sir?"

Marlene slammed a cupboard shut in the kitchen and Bull flinched. He could hear her coming toward the living room and his stomach began to burn. Poor Morrow, he thought, feeling suddenly sorry for the odoriferous professor. Maybe he could shuttle him through the front door before Marlene descended upon him with her Glade aerosol and sharp nails. Of course, if Bull had kept the promise he'd made to her that morning, Morrow wouldn't need rescuing. "That man is not, I repeat, not, to come into this house," she'd said. "Yes, honey," he'd said, "I mean it, Bull," she'd said, "I know," he'd said, "Promise," she'd said. And he'd promised. But there was Morrow. And here came Marlene.

She breezed by him before Bull had the chance to get up out of his chair. She walked straight toward Morrow, stopping in front of him with her hands on her hips. Bull sighed with relief: they were empty; balled into fists, but empty. She stared directly at Morrow, and though Bull could see only the back of her head, he knew exactly the expression on her face. It would be hard: her lips thin and mouth bending down at the edges, her eyes narrow slats and gone cold, the skin around her jaw drawn tight. Bull was familiar with the look; it was very unfriendly.

Morrow saw none of this. He was gormless, and greeted Marlene's odium with the smile of a child: teeth showing and eyes bright with innocence.

Poor bugger, Bull thought again. But Marlene didn't strike out, though she was more than capable. Instead she stepped to the window, and with one great heave hoisted the pane. She turned back to Morrow.

"Stuffy in here," she said. Then left the room.

Morrow had no idea of the danger he'd just faced. It was the second time that day he'd displayed what Bull thought to be a glaring lack of awareness. The professor had been equally oblivious out at the old quarry. Bull had tried to dissuade him from making the trek, but Morrow had been insistent. "I must see it, Mr Mayor," he'd said, "scientifically speaking, you understand." So Bull grudgingly accompanied him.

It was worse than minding a toddler. Several times Bull had to stop and take Morrow by the shoulders, look him in the face and slowly explain that he must be careful. "There are flues, shafts, all over," he'd said in a softly scolding voice, "and you can't see them. They're covered over with brush." There would be nothing he could do, he told Morrow, if he fell into one. And each time Morrow nodded like an imbecile, then started off again on his reckless wander.

When at last they made it safely to the quarry, Morrow paid so little attention to the crater that Bull could feel his face grow flush with anger. Instead, the professor stood with his back to the excavation and took in the surrounding forest. "Yes, I see," he said again and again, until Bull, his spleen gorged, blurted, "You're not even bloody looking at it!" But Morrow just smiled his stupid child's smile and said, "Oh, but I am."

He said nothing after that. Not a word, not until they had trudged all the way back to the house and Bull, knowing he shouldn't, knowing he'd promised, held the front door open and led Morrow through to the living room, where the man removed his shoes and parked himself, Indian fashion, on the sofa. Only then did he open his tight little mouth and tell Bull what he was thinking.

"Well, Mr Mayor?" Morrow said.

"Sorry?"

"No proposition for our dilemma?"

"I really don't think I follow you, Professor," Bull said.

"No," Morrow smiled, "I don't believe you do."

He pulled his feet from beneath him and slipped them into his tattered loafers. Then he stood up. "Not to worry," he said, offering Bull a feline grin. "I'll take care of the cordon myself, shall I?"

Marlene stirs, snorts softly and offers the slightly phlegmy cough her years of occasional smoking have bequeathed to her. Bull freezes, one leg in his trousers, the other crooked and ready to enter. He holds his breath. She rolls on to her side and stretches an arm out for his pillow, which she snatches greedily to her chest. But she is still asleep. At least until he pulls his undershirt over his head. Bull can feel her looking at him before he pushes his head through the neck-hole.

"Where do you think you're going?" she asks.

"Out." Bull smiles.

"It's three-thirty in the bloody morning."

"Yes."

"Get back into bed," Marlene growls, "and stop being so foolish."

Bull takes a breath, so deep it hurts his lungs, then doesn't know what to do with it. If he lets it slip out as a sigh, Marlene will think him insolent; if he blows it out in a burst, she'll take it as a challenge. Neither is agreeable to Bull. He winces at the strain, leans forward and releases the air through his nostrils, as slowly as he can.

"What was that?" Marlene blurts, pushing herself up.

"What?" Bull answers quickly, slipping a hand to his lower back. "Oh, nothing. Just a twinge in the old back, is all. Go back to sleep, honey."

"Don't honey me," Marlene snaps. "And get your ass back to bed."

"It's just," Bull stumbles, "I'm having trouble sleeping

again. A short walk to tire me out. I'll be back in ten minutes."
He smiles through the dark. "Promise."

Bull had been standing on Forsythe Street, outside the
Marbleton Municipal Building, when the old yellow school
bus pulled into town. He'd just given Janeane his scribbled
notes for a speech he was due to give at the monthly town
council meeting—on the merits of the pay-per-bag method of
garbage collection—so she could type them up. He'd once
before, in the early days of mayoralty, tried to read from his
own handwritten draft and the results had been disastrous. His
nearly illegible penmanship had produced numerous pauses,
and in the end, after apologizing for his error, he'd worked off
the top of his head, to similar effect. He'd learned his lesson.
Ever since, Bull had made certain that Janeane Pryor, his official assistant—as well as the unofficial assistant to all the other
council members—typed up a clean copy of his thoughts.
Which was not the easiest task, all things considered.

Bull had paused on the bottom step and was contemplating a
return to his office to clarify a few of the more muddled points of
the speech for Janeane when he saw it creep around the corner
onto Forsythe. To look at it, there was nothing very extraordi-
nary about the bus. A little long in the tooth, as such vehicles
go: the rear suspension all but given up the ghost and the requi-
site yellow faded and flaked; a long unfriendly dent along one
side, from just behind the door to the rear tire well. But it wasn't
so much the condition of the bus that caught Bull's attention—
and the attention of those Marbletonians who were making
their way along Forsythe to and from the stores downtown—as

it was the sound. The sound of singing. It seemed to precede the vehicle, to float out before it, announcing its arrival. To Bull it sounded almost like a hymn, like the softly reverential tones of a church choir. Yet there was something in the tone that was emphatically secular. He could not make out the lyrics, which were muted within the dimpled and scarred canary shell.

All those walking along Forsythe had stopped to watch the bus as it pulled up to the curb in front of the Municipal Building, in front of Bull. Even cars had pulled to the side of the street, their drivers craning to see what was happening.

Bull waited as the singing subsided. He could feel the sweat beginning to rise on his brow and moistening the cotton fabric of his golf shirt where it pinched tightly under his arms. The engine choked and sputtered, and finally died. Then the doors folded back and Bull could have sworn that, as they did so, he'd seen a small cloud of smoke billow forth.

As the bus emptied its load, Bull did not register faces; rather he saw nose rings, lip rings, eyebrow rings; shaggy hair, shorn hair, rainbow hair; combat fatigues, torn jeans, gypsy dresses. He saw backpacks, rucksacks and duffle bags; guitars, flutes and bongo drums.

And then, he saw Morrow. Standing there on the sidewalk in front of him. His hair bushier than ever; his beard scruffier; his eyes brighter, more mischievous, and lit with a defiance that was anything but childish.

"What's this?" Bull managed, feeling a little apprehensive at the sight of Morrow's fiery little grin.

"I told you I would take care of it, Mr Mayor," Morrow smiled. "And I will."

"Take care of what?"

"Why the cordon, of course." Morrow shook his head as if the answer was quite obvious.

Bull looked around him, at the strange bodies that had spilled onto the sidewalk, some already lounging on the steps of the Municipal Building, others mingling with his now-confused-looking constituents. Still others had wandered into the street, oblivious to any traffic, and stood gazing about themselves as if lost.

"I wish you'd told me," Bull said.

"Oh, Mr Mayor," Morrow said, clapping a bony hand on Bull's shoulder. "I'm sure you've got more pressing concerns, running the town and all."

"Not really," Bull said, trying his best to sound firm.

"Look." Morrow turned and made a wide sweeping gesture, taking in his flock. "We're just going to pick up a few supplies and then we'll be heading on out to get things set up."

"I don't know if this is such a good idea," Bull said, lowering his head. Then he caught wind of something and sniffed at the air. "Is that dope I smell?"

Morrow laughed his snorting, squeaking piglet laugh.

"Not to worry," he said. "Not to worry." Then he turned and began to gather his charges.

Bull watched as the strange crowd gathered around Morrow, swarming toward him as if he were a guru. He couldn't make out what was said, but heads nodded in unison as if an understanding had been reached. With another wave of his arms, Morrow had the rabble moving en masse along Forsythe Street toward the stores.

Halfway down the block, Morrow stopped and turned back to face Bull, who still hadn't moved from where he stood.

Morrow cupped his thin hands around his mouth and hollered in his piping pubescent voice:

"I forgot to tell you. I called the media."

Media? What media? Bull thought, but said nothing, already uncomfortable under the stares of his fellow citizens.

Bull is breathing heavily. The burning that has become commonplace in his belly has moved into his chest. His first thought is heart attack, and with it comes a brief but horrifying wave of terror. But his fright passes quickly as he recognizes the pain, recollects it as he would the face of a long-absent friend. It is the pain of exertion, the pleasant discomfort of athleticism. It has been years since he's felt it; many more years than he cares to admit. It belongs to a time of wind sprints and tackling dummies, of running stairs and hefting weights, of shouting crowds and sweetly curved cheerleaders. In his head the surging blood beats in time with the chant *toro, toro.* He wants to tell Darryl, but he's too far ahead, moving through the nighttime forest with an ease of which Bull is jealous.

They have left the truck about a mile up the road, pulled far off onto the shoulder, very nearly in the ditch. It was Darryl who suggested it, saying it would look less suspicious that way. Bull had wanted to ask his son why it was that they needed to avoid suspicion, wanted to know exactly what it was that they were planning to do, but he held his tongue. Before they'd left the house, after Bull had changed into his clothes and promised Marlene that he was just going out for a late-night, sleep-inducing stroll, Darryl had placed his hand on Bull's shoulder and said, "Trust me, Pop."

And Bull wanted to. His son had never asked this of him before, and he'd been touched. To have said anything after they pulled the truck over would have compromised that trust. So he remained silent and followed.

—∿—

"So explain it to me again," Marlene said, the serving spoon loaded with mashed potatoes hovering above her plate. "Tell me why there's a busload of hippies tramping through town?"

Bull swallowed carefully, easing the not-quite-chewed carrots down his throat. But Marlene slapped her potatoes down beside her roast beef and pointed the spoon at him before he could speak.

"Don't bother," she said. "The less I understand the better. That way when people come up to me on the street or, God forbid, when I'm at the A&P doing the shopping, I can just look at them and shrug. I can say, 'I don't know. I really don't. I think that maybe Bull has gone over the edge. If you ask me, I'd think twice when it comes around to the next election.' And I'll say that Bull. Don't think I won't."

He couldn't eat any more. Two bites into his dinner and he couldn't stomach the thought of even one more forkful. His belly was on fire. He looked toward the kitchen counter, to the bottle of Maalox, and wondered if this wasn't how a drunk felt, an addict: willing to pass on the opportunity of sustenance for the cool comfort of vice.

He'd tried his best to explain the arrival of the bus, of Morrow and his merry band. He told Marlene about the fish, the Jericho trout. He'd recounted, as best he could, the story Morrow had read to him from the aging text in his office.

About Sir Holyfield Lewis and his unfortunate demise. About the effect unbridled progress had on delicate ecosystems. About Billy Finnegan and the planned cordon. But all he'd received in return were blank stares. From Marlene, Darlene and Darryl. And it ruined his appetite and left him with an unquenchable thirst for his antacid.

"Are they real hippies?" Darlene asked, pushing her meat to the side of her plate. "I mean, like real honest-to-God hippies?"

"I don't know," Bull said, trying to smile.

"Because," she went on, "they told us that there aren't any hippies any more."

"Who told you that?" Marlene said through narrowed eyes.

"Mr Robertson, at school. My history teacher. He told us that there is no such thing as hippies any more. And that when there was hippies they were only in the United States and not in Canada."

"That's ridiculous," Darryl said through a mouthful of boiled cabbage.

"Well," Darlene shot back, "that's what he said."

"Since when have teachers known anything?" Darryl replied, refilling his mouth.

"So," Darlene said, looking at Bull. "Are they real hippies or not?"

"I don't know, honey," Bull said, feeling somewhat better that at least his family was having a conversation at the dinner table, even if it was somewhat fraught. "I don't think so."

Marlene huffed and let her fork clatter against her plate. She drew herself straight up in her chair and set her hands in her lap.

"Phyllis Richmond told me," she said, her voice clear and confident, "that they had bongo drums and guitars. If that doesn't make them real hippies, I don't know what does. And if you ask me, I think they should be rounded up and sent packing. And believe you me, I'm not the only one."

—⁂—

Through the trees he sees the familiar shape of the Streamliner, its burnished aluminum shell catching the faint moonlight and illuminating the small clearing in which it sits. Bull sits down on a stump to catch his breath. He's somewhat embarrassed. Not by his now-apparent unhealthiness, though it has come as something of a surprise to him. He always considered himself to be in fair condition. Sure, some of his youthful muscle had gone to fat, but that was to be expected with age. Still, most of his bulk remained firm, and his arms were thick in the biceps, not flabby but hard. The work he did in the garden kept them that way. He understands now, though, his hands clutching his knees, his shaking forearms supporting the heft of his upper body, that his weight is simply that: weight.

This, however, is not what has brought about the humiliation he can now feel colouring his cheeks. It's the sight of Billy Finnegan's trailer. From the moment they stepped into the inky woods at the roadside—the whole while he followed Darryl, tried to keep pace with him, with his head pounding and his sweat pouring, with his mind turning back on itself to a time when it and his body were both fresh and innocent, prepared to face a future of promise together— Bull had no idea where he was. And now, sitting on his stump, sucking in the cool night air like a greedy child, he feels foolish. He once knew the forest as intimately as he did the fine veins of Marlene's breasts. He no longer knows either.

"Pop. Hey, Pop?"

He hears Darryl's call, but cannot yet respond. A few more deep breaths.

"You okay there, Pop?" Darryl asks, coming up beside him and laying a gentle hand on the top of Bull's head.

"Sure, son," Bull pants. "Just a little winded, is all."

Not even breathing hard, he thinks. I can hardly move and he's not even breathing hard. Bull decides that he may have underestimated his son, and finds the thought pleasing.

"Well, come on then," Darryl says and takes Bull by the arm and helps him to his feet.

They move together across the brief clearing, Bull propped against Darryl, a wounded soldier in need of his comrade's assistance.

At the door of the trailer Darryl lets go of his father's arm, steadies him and offers him a look of condolence. An apology, it seems to Bull, for the strain he's put him through, but also for the strain that is to come. There is kindness in the boy's face and Bull wonders where exactly that comes from. Then Darryl turns to the door and knocks three times on the shiny metal. Three echoing reports that suggest a completely hollow interior.

The door opens without the least sound of movement from inside, as if Billy Finnegan was standing behind it, expecting visitors. Billy is wearing cut-off jean shorts and a slightly soiled dark green John Deere T-shirt. His short hair is mussed, but Bull can't tell whether from sleep or lack of combing. He suspects the latter.

"Hey there, Darryl," Finnegan says, as if a knock at his door in the middle of the night is normal.

"Billy."

"Howya doin', Bull?"

"Fine, Billy," Bull manages, his wind finally returning.

"Good to hear," Billy smiles. "What can I do for you boys?"

Even with his breath back, Bull feels a desperate need to sit down again, but there is something about the situation that keeps him from saying as much. He holds no rank in the circumstance, is very much the third party, standing on the fringe, waiting for an invitation to participate.

"Billy," Darryl says, his tone confidential, "you don't still have any of that stuff you salvaged from the old quarry depot, do you?"

Finnegan, hands on his hips and wide smile stretching his lips, says, "You know I do."

"Good," Darryl says, then turns to Bull. "You wouldn't mind if Pop and I borrowed a little something, would you?"

"Not one bit," Finnegan says, stepping back from the door. "Come on in. What's mine is yours."

It hadn't taken long for the complaints to start. At first they came by phone to Janeane Pryor at the Municipal Building. She wrote them all down, word for word, on small yellow Post-its and stuck them to Bull's desk. First just to the top, but when that was covered, she started sticking them to the edge, and before long the desk was ringed with a yellow fringe.

Standing in the doorway to Bull's office two weeks after Morrow and his coterie had arrived, Janeane smiled and said, "I like it. Looks a bit like a valance. Martha Stewart-ish."

Bull, in the midst of another bout of gastric discomfort, couldn't appreciate the humour. He'd started receiving phone calls at home, some coming late in the night, from constituents who demanded that he do something about the rabble out in the woods. Others had even come to the house and cornered him in the vegetable patch. He'd tried to convince them that what Morrow was doing was legal, that there was nothing that could be done. He'd been told as much by the sergeant at the OPP detachment in Brockton, who, after sending an officer out to check on things, told Bull that the police had better things to do with their time than harass campers.

Marlene was, of course, furious. She'd accused Bull of sitting idly by simply out of spite.

"You just want to embarrass me, don't you," she shouted at him the night before. "What have I done? Have I done something horrible to you? If you loved me you wouldn't put me through this kind of humiliation."

"Sweetheart," Bull said as soothingly as he could, "you have to understand. There's nothing I can do about it. I've tried."

"Well, you haven't tried hard enough."

"There really isn't anything —"

"What about Darlene?" Marlene interrupted, her voice gone cold. "Do you not even care about your own daughter?"

"What are you talking about?" Bull asked. "What about Darlene?"

"My God, Bull," Marlene said to him. "Are you blind as well as stupid? She goes out with them. Out there with those hippies."

"What do you mean? When?"

"At night. After we're in bed."

Bull felt like he'd been punched square in the middle of his burning belly. "How?" he wheezed. "How do you know?"

Marlene gave a contemptuous smirk and turned away from him. Over her shoulder she said, "I'm her mother. She *talks* to me."

The interior of Billy Finnegan's trailer home is impeccably tidy and Bull has trouble equating it with the slovenly man standing over the hot plate waiting for the water to boil. He half-expected fly-swarmed cases of empty beer bottles, even though he has never known Finnegan to be a drinker. He has his breath back and his chest has loosened but he still cannot get comfortable. The bench he's sitting on is narrow and his belly is pushed up tight against the table, but that's not it. It's the pressed wildflowers in picture frames that hang on the walls that have him feeling slightly off balance. He wants to ask Darryl about them.

"You take sugar d'you, Bull?" Finnegan asks, a spoonful hovering over the cup of instant coffee.

"No, Billy. Just milk is fine."

Bull notices as Finnegan adds two spoonfuls to Darryl's coffee without asking. He accepts his own cup with a smile, and after a sip, which feels like acid in his stomach, he gestures to the picture frames on the wall across from him.

"Those are nice," Bull says, trying to sound casual.

"Aren't they just," Finnegan says, looking proudly at the wall. "Darryl made them."

Bull looks at his son, who shyly lowers his head, but not quickly enough to hide his own satisfied grin.

"They're good, son," Bull says awkwardly, feeling immediately guilty for his artlessness.

"I been telling him that he should try to sell them at the craft shop in town." Finnegan smiles, handing Darryl his coffee. "But he don't listen to me."

Bull wants to say something else, but can't find the words. He wants to tell Darryl yes, Finnegan is right, he should try to sell his flowers, but he knows if he does, it won't come out right. Instead, he takes another sip of the corrosive coffee. He feels out of place here. Not unwelcome, just unprepared. Darryl rescues him with a clap on the back.

"How about we show Pop here the box, Billy."

"Sure thing," Finnegan says, setting his own cup on the table. "Got it right over here."

Finnegan goes to the far end of the trailer and pulls back the thin curtain that conceals the bed. Pushing the covers back, he grabs hold of the edge of the mattress and folds it over. He then lifts the lid of the storage well beneath and reaches in, taking out a small wooden crate, which he sets on the floor. After he's rearranged the bed, tucking the covers neatly under the mattress, he lifts the crate and places it gently on top.

"Well," he says brightly, "don't just sit there. C'mon over and have a peek."

Bull was sitting in his office peeling Post-its from his lamp when Janeane came in. She didn't knock, which was unusual. Even though Bull kept his door open, Janeane would always give a knock and wait for him to give her permission to enter.

Her just walking in and the strained look on her face told Bull that something was very wrong.

"What's up, Janeane?" Bull asked, hoping, though he felt guilty for doing so, that it was some Pryor family trauma.

"TV people," she said, her complexion blanched. "From the news. And that scientist fella."

"Oh, God. Where?"

Janeane walked quickly across the room to the window. With a quick jerk of the cord she pulled up the venetian blinds and pointed down to the front steps of the Municipal Building.

Bull did not want to get out of his chair, felt almost as if he couldn't. His legs like lead weights. But he pushed himself to his feet and went and stood behind Janeane and looked over her shoulder.

The steps below were crowded with Morrow's people, most of them lounging about, a few kicking a beanbag back and forth between them. On the sidewalk a short distance away, a small group of townsfolk were beginning to gather, looking with disgust between the scraggly haired bodies collected on the steps and the battered bus parked against the curb. How could he not have heard it pull up? Bull wondered. Then he noticed the white van from the television station parked behind the bus.

"They want you to go down," Janeane said, her voice no more than a whisper.

Bull took a deep breath and shrugged.

"Well, I guess I'd better," he sighed. "Who knows, maybe I'll become a star."

Janeane did not laugh, but followed him silently out of the office and toward the stairwell. Halfway down to the foyer she stopped him and straightened his collar and smoothed down his hair. Bull felt like a little boy on his way to get his class picture taken.

"Tell me, Janeane," he said. "What do you make of all this?"

She shook her head. "Fun's fun." She frowned. "But we don't need this."

"No, we don't," Bull agreed.

"And all over some silly fish."

"Yes," Bull said, turning back down the stairs. "A silly goddamn fish."

Morrow met him at the front door, his arms spread wide as if he was going to embrace him. Bull shrank back slightly, then Morrow clapped his hands together and rubbed them vigorously.

"It's wonderful, Mr Mayor. Absolutely wonderful." He looked quickly out toward the steps. "Of course I would have liked a somewhat larger media presence, but it's early days yet."

"I really don't know about this, Dr Morrow," Bull said sheepishly.

"Oh, don't be nervous, Mr Mayor," the professor chirped. "It'll be a piece of cake. You might even like it. Besides, if you don't mind, I'll do most of the talking. You know, scientific expertise and all that."

As Bull walked out onto the front steps of the Municipal Building he could feel the eyes settle upon him, especially those of his constituents, who, he could tell, even from a distance, were anything but pleased.

A woman in a close-fitting red jacket and skirt approached him and he immediately recognized her from the television. She smiled and introduced herself and Bull couldn't help but notice the heaviness of her makeup. Her hair also looked too dark to be natural. Behind her stood a slightly overweight man in a pair of oily jeans and a sweatshirt with the university's logo; he wore a baseball cap turned backward and balanced a large video camera on his shoulder. The reporter, who was still talking, though Bull hadn't heard a word she'd said, took him by the shoulders and shifted him slightly closer to Morrow, then she turned to the cameraman.

"Is that good?"

"Perfect," he said, holding up a thumb.

"Right," she said through unusually white teeth, "I'll just ask you two some questions and you just answer them. Don't worry if you stumble, we'll edit it all together when we get back to the studio. Just go with whatever thought you have. And we'll start with the professor, if you don't mind, Mr Mayor?"

Bull shook his head: "No, not at all."

Then a bright light affixed to the top of the camera came on and Bull shielded his eyes. The reporter gently pulled his hands away from his face.

"Sorry about that," she said apologetically. "It is a little intense but you'll get used to it."

"Now," she continued, holding her microphone at arm's length, "Professor Morrow, can you tell us what this is all about?"

"I can indeed," Morrow said, bouncing up and down on the balls of his feet. "Oh, yes. I can indeed. What's happened here in Marbleton is, I can safely say, a magnificent scientific marvel. A discovery, or rather a rediscovery, of stunning importance. I would put it on a par with the finding, in 1938, of the long-thought-extinct coelacanth . . ."

Just as Morrow started in on the story of Sir Holyfield Lewis, Bull caught sight of Darlene. He didn't recognize her at first; her usually straight, long blond hair was pulled up into untidy bunches on top of her head. She was standing at the bottom of the steps, partly hidden behind a tall lanky boy in a tie-dyed shirt with a banjo slung across his shoulders. Having been spied by her father, she tried to shield herself from view. Then, with an expression of boldness Bull had never seen before, she forced herself into the open and very obviously took the arm of the scraggly troubadour. Bull could feel himself cringe when Darlene, looking straight at him, stretched onto her tiptoes and sucked on the boy's earlobe. It was as if through a long cardboard tube that he heard the reporter's next question to Dr Morrow.

"And just what exactly is it that you plan to do here, Professor?"

Bull could feel Morrow's spindly arm brush against his own as it shot into the air.

"We're going to fight!" the fishy-scented aquatic biologist squealed.

"What?" Bull said in disbelief.

"Fight how?" the reporter eagerly asked.

"We're going to take a stand in the forest," Morrow said, his tone verging on rabid. "We'll defend the Jericho trout from the manic industrialization that's intent on wiping it from the face of the earth. To the last person we'll defend it."

A loud shout rose from the steps, and looking out Bull could see the Marbletonians standing on the fringe of the crowd begin to slink away, frightened by the scene. Then he heard the reporter.

"Mr Mayor? Mayor Maxim?"

"Yes?" Bull said, still stunned by Morrow's outburst.

"As the authority in the town, what do you plan to do about this incendiary demonstration?"

"Incendiary?"

"Yes, Mr Mayor," the reporter smiled, looking hungrily at Bull. "By the sound of things, this is a protest that could easily become violent."

"Violent?" Bull said, shaken. "I don't know. I don't know what Dr Morrow is talking about. We don't have any industry here. We don't even have any police."

Another shout went up from the crowd.

The reporter turned to the cameraman and drew a finger across her throat.

"Perfect," she said to him, then turned back toward Bull and Morrow. "Thank you very much, gentlemen. That'll play great. We're just going to get a few shots of the crowd now, if you don't mind."

Bull felt a spidery hand crawl across his shoulder.

"Oh, boy," Morrow said, his grin wildly boyish. "I think that went great, just great. Didn't you, Mr Mayor?"

Bull pushed his hand roughly away.

"No, sir," he said, feeling his guts start to bubble. "No, sir, I didn't think it went just great at all."

"You're not upset about all that making-a-stand stuff, are you, Mr Mayor?" Morrow said, the picture of innocence. "That was just for the camera. We're in this together, you and I. We're going to put this place on the map."

"I'll have you know," Bull said, turning back into the building, "that Marbleton is already on the map."

Then he stopped and looked back toward the crowd in search of Darlene, but she was nowhere to be seen.

Bull cannot believe what he is seeing. The lid is off the crate. Inside there is straw, old and dry. The first thing that comes to his mind when he looks at it is Marlene's hair after she's had it permed and dyed. So brittle that just touching it might cause the strands to snap. Then Bull sees the pale pink sticks. He counts six of them, nestled in among the straw, but there might be more buried beneath.

"Jesus Christ, Billy. How long have you had this stuff?"

Finnegan smiles proudly: "Oh, it's gotta be going on six years now. But I'm sure it's been kicking around a whole lot longer than that."

Bull has to suppress the urge to flee, to run home blindly out of the trailer in search of safe cover.

"Do you know how dangerous this is?" Bull asks in lieu of flight.

Finnegan, still holding the lid of the crate, turns it over in his hands and holds it up so Bull can read it.

"Says to keep it in a cool, dry place. I figure under the bed's the closest I got." Then he laughs. "Hell, I figure if it ain't gone off yet, it's not going to."

"And this was just sitting over there at the quarry?"

"Yep. Found it in one of the old depot sheds out back of the wash house."

"Don't sweat it, Pop," Darryl says, putting a hand on Bull's shoulder and giving it a squeeze. "We'll be rid of it soon enough."

Darryl's touch is comforting, and Bull can feel his fright slipping away. It's as if their roles have been reversed and his son has become the paternal rock. And Bull wonders if Darryl begrudges him for never having been that rock for him.

"You all right there, Pop?" Darryl asks, leaning in toward him with an expression of genuine concern.

"Sure, son," Bull says. "It's just my stomach. It's goddamn killing me."

The weight of the mayoral chain felt like a lodestone around his neck. Looking out at the gallery from his seat in the middle of the horseshoe-shaped council table was like looking out at the assembled guests of an unpopular marriage. On one side were his stern-faced constituents; on the other, Morrow and his quite obviously light-headed supporters. And the aisle running down the middle might as well have been a sweeping gorge for all the chance there was of one side reaching out toward the other. If they had rocks, Bull thought, they would probably be throwing them at one another.

The question had just been put to him, from the constituency camp, why the authorities hadn't been called and these rabble-rousers run clear out of town. Before Bull could answer, a chorus of hisses and barely stifled profanities rose from Morrow's crew. Bull had to bang his gavel to quiet them.

"As I told you before," Bull said, leaning in close to the microphone which he normally didn't have to use, since very rarely did anyone bother showing up for the council meetings, "the land that Professor Morrow and his supporters are . . ." He hesitated. "The land that Professor Morrow and his supporters are . . . occupying . . . is still owned by NystroCorp. And the police told me that if NystroCorp didn't launch a complaint, then there was nothing that could be done. Now I spoke to Robert Nystrom himself this afternoon and he told me . . ."

Bull searched the table for the note he'd made that afternoon. Having found it, he took a good few moments to decipher his own handwriting.

"He told me," Bull continued, feeling a little flustered, "to quote his exact words: 'I don't give a damn who's in that forest. It could be the Queen of Sheba for all I care. Just don't be calling me about any freaking lawsuits. We got signs up all over the place, and if those bastards can't read, then that's just too damn bad.'"

Bull folded the paper into quarters and set it down on the table beside the pitcher of water that he so desperately wanted a drink from.

"So you see," he went on, feeling more parched with every word, "if Bob Nystrom and his brother don't want them moved, I'm afraid there's nothing we can do."

Another shout went up, this time from both sides, and Bull had to hammer his gavel again. As he did, he saw Morrow, who was sitting right up front, slowly get to his feet and raise his hand, as if he were a schoolboy waiting to be called upon.

Bull made to look away, but the professor had already caught his eye.

"Yes, Dr Morrow?" Bull said, defeated.

"I was wondering if I might say a few words?"

A low grumble started on the Marbletonian side of the gallery, and a councillor to Bull's left began to object, but Bull held out a hand to silence him.

"I figure," Bull said diplomatically, "that since Dr Morrow is the reason we're all here, we might as well do him the courtesy of hearing what he has to say."

"How very kind of you, Mr Mayor," Morrow said and performed an awkward bow in Bull's direction. Then he turned slightly and faced the constituents.

"I fear," he began in a vain attempt to lower the pitch of his voice, "that we have gotten off on the wrong foot. It was never my intention, never our intention, to cause you any distress. I realize we may"—he made a wide, arcing gesture, which took in those sitting around him—"appear slightly odd to you. We're not, how should I say, a very tidy bunch. But I implore, don't let our aspect prejudice you against us. We've come here only to do good. You have, in the vicinity of this fine town—and I don't mean to be patronizing, for I think this is indeed a very fine town. You have in the vicinity a true marvel, nay a wonder. It should be cherished. But to be cherished it must be protected. And that is all we aim to do. Protect. We are not against you. We are for you. So, please, I beg you: accept us. Think of us not as interlopers, but rather guardians. Your guardians. Guardians of your precious wonder."

Finished, Morrow executed another clumsy bow.

Then someone at the rear of the gallery shouted, "Why don't you just fuck off out of here, you hippie bastard."

There was a moment of complete and stunned silence as the profanity sank in, then the room exploded, both sides screaming obscenities and jabbing fingers in the air. Bull pounded his gavel, hit it so hard against the table that the head came off and clattered across the floor. Still there was disorder. And it began to appear as if something truly ugly was about to occur. Then, through the chaos, Bull could hear a lone voice begin to chant. At first he couldn't make out what was being said, just the simple rhythm of the cadence, but he recognized the voice. He stretched himself on tiptoes to get a better look. People in the gallery were out of their chairs now and the two sides were pushing dangerously close. Then the chant started to catch on with Morrow's people, and as it did, the constituents grew quieter. That's when Bull saw her. Darlene, right in the middle of the throng, leading the mantra, her fist pumping in the air.

"Hell no, we won't go."

She was looking straight at him, her grubby balladeer at her side, banging time on the skin of his banjo.

"Hell no, we won't go."

The chant grew louder still, and Darlene began to push her way into the aisle, pulling the banjo player behind her. Fist still stabbing the air, she formed the head of the parade, leading the filthy chorus down the middle of the gallery to doors at the far end, and from there, out into the streets.

This time he hadn't fallen behind, hadn't felt old and out of breath. This time Bull kept pace. A young man again, rushing the line, stiff-arming the low-slung branches. He'd even, in a moment of bravado, offered to carry the crate, but Darryl kindly waved him off, saying that he and Finnegan would share the load.

"I have to give him something to hold on to," Darryl had said, "or else he gets lost."

For all their weight, his and Darryl's, and Finnegan's notorious clumsiness, they'd made very little noise as they wound their way through the woods. Whatever sound they did make was easily drowned out by the noises of the night creatures hiding in the darkness. Twice Darryl had halted their progress, putting a protective arm across Bull's chest. It was as if he knew instinctively where the flues were. And as they drew near to their destination, Darryl guided Bull and Finnegan with such care and paternal concern that once again Bull felt as if he were the son, and it made him feel so happy that he thought he might actually cry.

Bull hadn't asked Darryl exactly what they were going to do, and Darryl hadn't offered. But once he had taken a good look at the ancient sticks of dynamite that Finnegan had salvaged from the old quarry, it was plainly obvious, and he decided simply to trust his son.

Now, though, standing in the brief clearing at the edge of the quarry, Bull is beginning to have doubts, which are accompanied by a painful flare of indigestion.

"You know, Darryl," he says. "I'm not so sure about this."

Even in the dark he can tell his son is disappointed,

"Well, Pop," Darryl says quietly. "It's up to you, really. If you don't want to do it, we won't do it."

It's like a hot poker pushing at him from the inside. He wants so badly to please his son but he's . . . he's what? What is it that's keeping him from doing what his darling boy wants? Why is it that he can't give Darryl just this one thing? And finally, in a flash, as if he's known all along, Bull realizes what it is that's stopping him. What it is that always stops him. He's afraid. He's afraid of what people will say, afraid of what Marlene will say. He's afraid of Morrow and his unwashed horde. He's afraid of his constituents. He's afraid of getting caught. He's afraid Darlene won't love him any more.

"Darryl," he whispers. "What about Darlene?"

"What about her?"

"This will break her heart."

He hears Darryl laugh.

"Is that it, Pop? Is that what you're worried about?"

He can't remember the last time he's heard Darryl laugh.

"What?" Bull says and hears his own voice crack. "What is it that's funny?"

"You think Darlene cares about some stupid fish?"

"But . . ."

"It's not the fish, Pop."

"But she's out there," Bull says, his tone now panicky. "She's out there in the woods with those . . . with those . . . people."

"Sure she is, Pop. But that doesn't have anything to do with the fish."

"It doesn't?"

"No."

"Really?"

"Really."

Bull feels as if he doesn't know anything any more. Nothing makes sense to him.

"So," says Darryl, coming closer. "Do you want to do this or not?"

Out of the darkness Bull hears a noise. Strange. Out of place here in the woods. At first he cannot make it out. Not crickets. Not critters in the underbrush. Not the wind. It's something more melodious, like singing.

And it is singing. Faint and hymn-like. And there's something else, something straining just beneath the song: a banjo.

He turns to Darryl.

"Yes," he says. "Yes, I want to do this."

"Well, hot dog," chirps Finnegan. Bull had forgotten he was with them.

He feels Darryl press the dry stick into his hand and then the flame of the lighter lights up his son's face.

"The wick, it'll be pretty dry, Pop. So you better throw it as soon as it catches."

He watches as the small yellow flame licks the fuse and waits for it to ignite.

"What if it doesn't work?"

"Relax, Pop," Darryl says confidently. "It'll work."

And with that the fuse sparks to life, and Bull is reminded of the sparklers he used to buy for Darryl and Darlene when they were still children and how they used to run through the backyard writing their names in the air.

"Come on, Bull," Finnegan yells out of the darkness. "Get rid of the thing."

And Bull draws his arm back, feeling the stretch in his pectorals and the wound-up elastic tension of the tendons in his elbow. He plants one foot firmly on the ground in front of him and pushes off hard with the other. His arm begins an exquisite arc, starting from behind his head and extending upward. At the zenith his fingers open and he feels the stick of dynamite leave his hand and watches as it soars out into the air before him, out and out, a perfect toss, the sparkling fuse spitting needles of brightness into the black night. For a moment it seems to pause, suspended in the void, as if hanging from a string, before it begins its descent, falling, falling into the chasm, its glittering ember growing dimmer and dimmer until it disappears. There is utter silence. Even the far-off singing has stopped.

Then the night roars with great force and Bull falls backward, landing with such a thump that he bites a chunk out of the tip of his tongue. But he is laughing. Even as the blood starts to stain his lip, he is laughing, thinking of the fish, the Jericho trout, its muscles as stiff as a board as it sinks to the bottom of the quarry.

He can hear Darryl's voice close to his ear, and though he's yelling, he sounds far away.

"Pop? Pop? You okay?"

"Great," Bull hears himself slur, swollen tongued. "Oh, boy. I'm just great. It was just like an open-field tackle."

With Darryl's help, he pulls himself to his feet.

"You're bleeding," Darryl says, sounding much closer now.

"Yes, I am, son. Yes, I am." Then he takes his son's face in his hands. It's been so long, so long since he's reached out and touched him the way he's so wanted to. "Do you know what kind of fish drowns, Darryl?" he says, feeling so happy, so much happier than he has in more years than he can remember. "Do you, son?"

He can feel Darryl shaking his head.

"One that's too afraid to swim," Bull shouts out and looks up to the night sky, laughing. "That's what kind. One that is too goddamned afraid to swim."